NICOT

Queen Rearing

2nd Edition

The Non-Grafting Method

For Raising Local Queens

Grant F. C. Gillard

NICOT Queen Rearing

2nd Edition

The Non-Grafting Method

For Raising Local Queens

by Grant F. C. Gillard

For more information:

Grant F.C. Gillard
1259 SW 600th Rd
Holden, MO 64040-9103
grantfcgillard@gmail.com

Grant F.C. Gillard is a Presbyterian Pastor and Beekeeper. He has been keeping bees since 1981. He speaks at bee conferences and conventions across the nation. Contact him at **grantfcgillard@gmail.com** to check his availability for your next event.

You can find more information about the author at the conclusion of this book, or www.grantgillard.weebly.com

Dedication

I dedicate this book to Cory Stevens of Dexter, Missouri, where he lives with his wife, Jaime, along with their two children, Camden Lane and Jade Olivia.

This book is dedicated in honor of Cory's successful completion (on the first attempt) of the E.A.S. Certified Master Beekeeper in the summer of 2013.

Cory is a phenomenal queen breeder, teacher, and rising star on the apicultural horizon. He generously shares his queen rearing wisdom in his affable, gregarious manner.

Cory has found a way to make his system work and he's not worried about keeping it a secret.

I count it an honor, as do many other beekeepers, just to hang around him and profit from his knowledgeable and insightful expertise.

Cory is a blessing, as is his family. I cherish his friendship and collegiality, as well as the many ways he tacitly challenges me to excellence with the high standards he brings to his personal life in addition to keeping honey bees.

Acknowledgements

No author produces a book in a vacuum.
I'm grateful to the many beekeepers, both still living and many who are now deceased, who came along side of me in my times of need, rectified my crippling ignorance and redirected my overly idealistic zeal. They graciously answered my unremitting questions, and patiently put up with my incessant ruminations of supposedly better and theoretically innovative ways to keep honey bees.

Author's Notes to the 2nd Edition

The NICOT non-grafting system of queen rearing has been an absolute "game changer" to the ways I keep honey bees and produce honey. I firmly believe queen rearing, and one's opportunity to raise their own queens, opens more doors than any other skill in this ever-changing endeavor of beekeeping, irrespective of one's experience, or the lack of it.

The NICOT method removes the barriers of learning how to graft and simplifies the identification of age-appropriate larvae to produce the best, optimally raised queen honey bees.

Other Popular Beekeeping Resources by

Grant F. C. Gillard

Available on amazon.com

Beekeeping with Twenty-five Hives:
From Passion to Profits

A Ton of Honey:
Managing Your Hives for
Maximum Production

Free Bees!
The Joy and the Insanity of Removing and
Retrieving Honey Bee Swarms

Keeping Honey Bees and Swarm Trapping:
A Better Way to Collect "Free" Bees

Sustainable Beekeeping:
Surviving in an Age of CCD

Backyard Beekeeping #1
What to Expect When You're Expecting Honey Bees

Backyard Beekeeping #3
Stepping Into Your Second Year

Backyard Beekeeping #5
The Five-Minute Queen Rearing Method

Innovative Beekeeping
A Radical Journey on a Road Less Traveled

Some of my hives in Mississippi County, in the Bootheel
region of Southeast Missouri, foraging on soybeans.

NICOT Queen Rearing
2nd Edition

Table of Contents

A Caveat:

A caveat is nothing but an admonition, kind of a velvet-lined caution, a gentle warning, a word to the wise, so to speak. So let me share a little caveat as you start reading this manuscript.

Queen rearing is not just about the bees. It's also about you. It's about your hopes and dreams, your aspirations as a beekeeper, and what level you may want to take your passion. Queen rearing will also test your patience as there are no short-cuts.

Queen rearing is a philosophy; it's about possessing a vision and being possessed by that vision. It's about creating a greater sense of autonomy and independence, believing in the potential of our on-going efforts, redefining and realigning the destiny of our colonies.

Raising your own queens is not hard work, but if you're like me, you'll find it challenging. It takes effort, dedication, commitment, and the consuming faith that says *you can do this*. Every step in this process will test your resolve. You will be tempted to quit and fall back on easier ways. Only the strong need apply. Only the determined last.

Well, okay. It's not quite that dramatic. Just keep in mind that queen rearing, like most things in beekeeping, is simple, but it's not easy. The bees will often reveal how they have a mind of their own, and as we often find ourselves saying, "The bees don't read our books."

I've lost track of the hundreds of beekeepers who have asked me, "Why are my bees doing (fill in the blank with your confounding dilemma)? In many cases, I have no answer other than, "Beekeeping remains a mystery." Which is a fancy way of saying, "Beats me."

Rather than sound overly pretentious, I do like to add, "There's always a reason why bees do what they do. Sometimes we have to simply trust their judgment and follow their lead."

My encouragement is simply this: jump in and give it your best shot, but don't give up too soon if success initially eludes you. You'll find the desired results will come, eventually, and the end gains are well worth the persistent toil and perceived hardship. Just don't fool yourself into believing you'll find miraculous results the first time you give it a try.

But don't rule it out, either. I like to believe that the race is not always won by the swift, nor does the battle always favor the strong, brilliant people don't always find wealth, and the homecoming queen doesn't always win the heart of the starting quarterback. We all have our days when everything works out despite our limitations and inexperience.

I had an uncle who is now deceased who liked to say, "Some days you win; some days you lose. Some days you get rained out. But you still suit up for every game."

I'm not sure where that came from, but it certainly applies to beekeeping, especially about suiting up.

I also want you to remember two things as you venture forth into queen rearing. First, T. Alan Armstrong advises, "Champions do not become champions when they win the event, but in the hours, weeks, months and years they spend preparing for it." Queen rearing takes practice. Skills are honed by repetition.

Second, remember these paraphrased words of Kahil Gibran, "The significance of a person is not what they attain, but rather in what they long to attain." Queen rearing also takes perseverance. It comes to those who really want to learn it.

Decide. Commit. Succeed. Rinse and repeat.

One more last thing. Much of my writing is not just about how I do things. I want you to understand why I do things the way I do them. I like to believe I have some method to my madness. You'll find me waxing poetically and effusing philosophically when you may just want me to get the show on the road.

I also do not possess the unwarranted hubris to believe I have the last word on any topic. Things change. I've changed. Your situation and circumstances will undoubtedly, be quite different than mine.

That said, what remains is my greatest hope for your success and enjoyment in keeping honey bees, regardless of your experience or level of involvement.

Like some starving beggar, I discovered where to find food. I share it so you won't have to be hungry, either.

All my best to your success.

Preface: Why This Book?

A long time ago, I decided I wanted to raise my own queen honey bees. It was about the time my beekeeping hobby started to move out of the limits of my backyard and into the realm of providing a potential return on my investment. If you keep bees, you know the investment is substantial. You also comes to accept the return on that investment is often dangling in the realm of "potential."

My initial motivation was based on imagining the money I could save raising my own queens instead of buying mail-order queens from the large commercial producers. I also longed for the convenience of having queens available when I needed them instead of making fifteen phone calls and listening to a supplier complaining about my small order and how much the shipping was going to cost. Thankfully, a lot of the logistics of shipping live queens has changed since then.

I also coveted an imagined margin of control on choosing which queens would provide the genetics that resulted in the beneficial qualities of my future hives. While most beginners hope for "gentle" bees, I was looking for winter survivability and honey production. I thought I could simply select for these traits. Varroa resistance wasn't even on the radar in those days. We were all pretty much treatment-free beekeepers back then.

Knowing the queen is the genetic custodian of the hive, I felt like I could breed queens and tailor my intentions like someone with a pedigreed dog who has great hopes selling registered puppies.

Well, it's not that easy. I still had a lot to learn. My apicultural education was lacking, particularly in the basic fundamentals of honey bee biology. Those were the boring chapters in the beginning beekeeping books I skipped over to get to the good stuff, like harvesting honey.

Despite by grand schemes, there were two things holding me back from raising my own queens. Queen rearing seemed to hold a mystique accessible only to the experienced beekeepers who knew how to crack the secret code.

Additionally, the skill required to raise queens was cloaked in the clandestine terminology circling around an unfamiliar word: "grafting." I had no idea what grafting was or how to do it, but it sounded like something above my pay grade.

Despite my hopes, I resigned myself to buying queens from commercial producers. At that time, that wasn't such a bad way to go for a beekeeper of my size and experience.

Then on one cold day in late January, accompanying the long anticipated "swimsuit" edition of Sports Illustrated magazine, one of the catalogs from a beekeeping supply company arrived in the mail.

To a beekeeper, these catalogs rival our fondest, childhood memories of when the hefty Sears Christmas catalog arrived and we spent countless hours after school, splaying out on the family room rug, coveting the toys Santa Claus might bring us.

Beekeeping catalogs have captured that same focus for me, though Santa has since informed me I'm now responsible for financing the purchase my choice of toys. Nonetheless, ask any experienced beekeeper and they'll tell you they still meticulously peruse the pages, not for what they need, but for what they don't have.

I wonder if some still splay themselves out on the family room rug or if the recliner is the preferred spot for reading. Personally, I prefer the kitchen table as I tend to fall asleep in the recliner, and more so if the television is on.

On this particular day when that fateful issue of beekeeping gadgets arrived, the pages flipped open to something I had not seen before: a kit to raise queens that did not require grafting. It was under the brand name of NICOT. I still had no concept of what it meant to graft, but if non-grafting meant I didn't need to do it, I felt I was half-way to raising my own queens.

My mind raced with the possibilities. I smelled potential and inhaled deeply. I imagined the autonomy of taking my hobby to that next level. Fueled by my desires to start raising queens, I filled out the order form, wrote out my check, peeled off a stamp and drove directly to the post office to slide that envelope in the outgoing mail.

I told you this was a long time ago.

When my NICOT kit arrived, I opened the box and spread out the contents on the kitchen table. I first noted the plethora of multiple parts in their respective plastic bags, all shiny and new. Then the alarming absence of any instructions on how these things fit together hit me right between my eyes.

My heart sank with the feeling things had already started to go south. After a few minutes of quiet, prayerful contemplation, I went on the Internet. Thankfully, no one else was using the phone, and after five minutes of waiting for my dial-up connection to go through, I found a resource that looked like the solution to my problem, an instructional VHS tape on the NICOT system.

I pulled out a fresh envelope and wrote the check. E-commerce was not yet perfected and every news outlet screamed about the dangers of providing your credit card information to the free-wheeling world-wide web. It's funny how just a few years later, our comfort level is such that we divulge all kinds of sensitive information and don't even think about the potential ramifications.

Three interminable weeks later, a package arrived in the mail in a discrete, plain, brown wrapper.

Well, it wasn't quite as helpful as what I needed. In that video presentation, because of a long, rainy spell during the production schedule, the author shows a picture of some hives and provides a lengthy voice-over that narrates the last half of the queen rearing process, which is probably the most critical part of the NICOT system.

So I just decided I had no choice but to do the best I could under the circumstances, and hoped somehow I might figure things out.

To cut to the chase, my NICOT experience proved to be very challenging, and was not meeting my goals. It was a total failure. I felt like a total failure. So much for good common sense.

Over the years, since writing my first edition, I have had a number of people tell me they invested the money in acquiring the NICOT kit, but never found the courage to move forward and actually raise their own queens. Staring at the contents of the kit was simply too intimidating and too complex. "It would have helped to have instructions," they lamented.

The lack of instructions was one of the motivating factors that that prompted me to write this book. The other factor was the number of times I thought I knew what I was doing, when in fact, I had no clue and had nowhere to turn to find out why I was continually striking out. Over the years, people sought me out complaining about making the same mistakes I made. I felt a calling to provide some relief.

With the purchase of this kit, there was a distinct absence of how to use it. In those early years, I could not find any helpful material online on how to overcome some of the shortcomings of the kit. Additionally, I didn't have the money for the therapy to overcome my own shortcomings. I chose, instead, to work through the process, but sheer persistence wasn't the answer. Ample profanity didn't seem to make any difference either.

But hold on! Let's be honest with each other. Isn't it just easier, more convenient and definitely less complicated to simply make a phone call to any one of a hundred southern, commercial queen producers and purchase a mail-order queen?

Yes, it is. But there are benefits of control and autonomy that I saw as something I wanted, something money could not buy but something I could find by raising my own queens. If I could just figure it out.

Eventually, I did, but not without that ample profanity I mentioned earlier.

Chapter One:

More To Saving Money
Than Saving Money

The primary reason expressed by the majority of beekeepers wanting to raise their own queens is, "to save money."

I'll bet you never saw that reason coming! It may be why you picked up this book.

As you read on, you'll see it is, definitely, quite possible to save money, perhaps quite a bit of money, by raising your own queens, season after season.

But more than saving money, you'll be able to select (within reason) the favorable traits of the queens you raise, and more importantly, you'll be able to control the quality of the queens in how they are produced and raised.

The secret to raising high quality queens is not just in the genetics, but how the larvae are chosen and fed. It takes an excessively large population of healthy nurse bees to provide enough nourishment (royal jelly) to produce high quality queens.

Despite the research and academic studies that prove what I just wrote, there are still newer, and surprisingly older, beekeepers who still believe in the sufficiency of just putting two frames of bees and open brood in a nuc box and letting them do their thing. Yeah, you'll get a queen or two, but I could speculate that these queens lack the vitality and longevity that I seek in my honey production.

That said, I used to think this practice was sufficient because I was insanely cheap. But then again, I had no real world experience to recognize a high quality queen and the potential she held for my operation. I still had much to learn about honey bee biology.

Additionally, you will control the availability of young queens when you want them. There are benefits beyond saving money--benefits money can't buy.

What you will find, however, is a trade-off between saving money against...

> ✓ the cost of the Nicot, queen rearing
> kit, plus tax and shipping, and the

time to learn the idiosyncrasies of the kit and how it works, not just the way you think it is *supposed* to work,

✓ the expenditure of your time and energy manipulating your colonies,

✓ a crash-course education in honey bee biology, accepting the fact you have a lot to learn about honey bee biology,

✓ a dedication to the discipline of maintaining an unforgiving schedule,

✓ a time of questioning your own sanity,

✓ the disappointment of your raised expectations thinking this method is no big deal, how even a caveman could raise queens this way,

✓ the regret of not taking your bee club's seminar on grafting and understanding the Doolittle method of queen-rearing,

✓ the persistence of all your buddies in the bee club who are thinking you'll supply them with gobs of cheap queens at a moment's notice,

- ✓ frequent outbursts of frustration, including the potential for mild profanity bouncing off the tree tops, with the gratitude you are all alone in your apiary,

- ✓ a moment or two of weeping and gnashing of teeth, replete with gnarled fists and a knotted stomach,

- ✓ and the price of your laziness or simple ignorance if you so choose to procrastinate.

And I am not sympathetic: procrastination is a choice, a very expensive choice in the realm of queen-rearing. If habitual procrastination is a problem for you, put this book down, now. Give this book to someone who is willing to pay the price of the discipline it takes to raise queen honey bees. Don't tell me I didn't warn you. Once you get rolling, you must stay on schedule.

Chapter Two:

Queen Rearing is a Challenge; Prepare for It

In the process of learning how to raise my own queens, some questions danced around my brain. Was raising my own queens worth the effort? Was this practice a good use of my time and energy? Was the tediousness of queen rearing something I was willing to endure and what was I going to receive for the inconvenience of learning how to raise my own queens? Would the process get easier?

There were numerous times, particularly in the early stages of my education, that calling up a queen producer was a preferred path of least persistence, the road of least resistance. Something kept telling me to give it another try.

In business, project managers forecast the "cost:benefit" ratio before undertaking any endeavor. Everything has a cost. The million dollar question becomes: do the benefits merit all the costs, irrespective if those costs come in time, money, energy, human personnel resources, retraining employees with new skills, opportunity costs, or tying up machinery that could be used for more profitable products that are more easily marketed?

The question can also be stated, "Is the gain worth the pain?" In this instance, I think it is, but often my results are not experienced immediately and the required effort is questioned. Faith in the process gives me patience for the long-term benefits of the short-term pain. Pain is the sacrifice for the greater good.

Eric Thomas, the "Hip Hop Preacher," says,

> *"If you aren't feeling the pain, you're not making the sacrifice. You will only be successful when you turn your pain into greatness, when you allow your pain to push you from where you are to where you want to be. Pain is part of the process. I challenge you to push yourself."*

Queen-rearing is challenging, but so is beekeeping in general, and these are challenging times to keep honey bees. New beekeepers fizzle out like fireworks in a thunderstorm. Both beekeeping and queen-rearing take work, commitment, and a strict attention to details.

My encouragement is to persevere through those challenges, push back against those obstacles. Greater rewards are just ahead, but you won't find them up ahead if you quit now.

However, to stay on the safe side, don't let your subscription to *Bee Culture* or *The American Bee Journal* expire. Not everyone is successful at queen-rearing on the first attempt; some not successful on their tenth attempt.

You may find yourself looking up some of the advertisers in those respective magazines, making a few phone calls to purchase queens if you get to that point of giving up or you find yourself pressed for time toward the end of the season.

My consistent advice is don't give up too early. Let those magazines be your back up plan, your Plan B. Everyone needs a Plan B, but don't forget why Plan A was your Plan A.

Do you remember the 1984 movie, "The Natural," a baseball movie with Robert Redford and Wilford Brimley? Brimley plays the part of Pop Fisher, the beleaguered manager, who mutters incessantly in the dug out and says, "Mother always wanted me to be a farmer."

There's always something we'd rather be, or do, and queen rearing will test that mettle. Queen rearing is a unique endeavor. It's not the easiest craft to learn.

On one hand, I am surprised how many beekeepers do not raise their own queens. But on the other hand, when I discovered the hours required of me to master the challenges, I have reversed my opinion. I now understand why many beekeepers prefer to purchase mail-order queens. It's just easier. I fully empathize with those beekeepers who sigh, "I just didn't have the time." Time is a very precious commodity. I get it.

But, as I'll explain, I did not want to be like everyone else. I did not enjoy subjecting myself to the variables of purchasing mail-order queens. I wanted to learn how to raise my own queens and rise above the normal way of doing things.

So I bought a NICOT queen-rearing kit, and jumped right in raising queens. I thought my results would come easy, like, there's nothing to this, right? There's no grafting involved. *It's gotta be easy!*

But I was wrong. It was painful and ripe with failure and frustration in those first attempts. It didn't get any better by the tenth attempt. I was humiliated by this little plastic box. It embarrassed me. I embarrassed myself with my choice of expletives. I wanted to quit. It was all pain and no gain. I was tempted to quit.

Quoting Eric Thomas, again, he says, "This is a soft generation. You quit on everything."

He also said, "Pain, is to be able, at any moment, to sacrifice what you are for what you will become."

So I sacrificed my pride, set aside my anger and frustration, and kept trying to find a path forward. I really did not want to continue buying mail-order queens. Accepting Plan B was not what I wanted to do, or become. And if Plan C was back yard chickens, I wasn't going there. And even my wife didn't want me going there despite the fresh eggs.

Keep in mind, however, it's always too early to give up, though your head and your heart tell you it's the easier, more pleasant thing to do. The long-term benefits, though they are the epitome of delayed gratification, are worth the short-term pain.

I'll say it again. Pain is the sacrifice for the greater good. But if you've ever experienced the pain and frustration trying to teach your 4-year old child how to tie their shoe laces, you'll readily opt for your back up plan: shoes with Velcro® straps. There is no shame in a child with Velcro® straps.

But if you can work through the frustration of teaching your child to tie their shoes, you are in the running for "Parent of the Year." And you have earned my highest respect.

That same ideal is why I kept forging ahead to perfect this infuriating contraption, but there were days I'd prefer to teach my kids how to tie their shoe laces than try, again, to get my NICOT kit to produce queens for me.

If you find yourself frustrated with your lack of success in queen-rearing, you may benefit from drawing a compromise with your aspirations. I would suggest continuing with your existing method of meeting your needs, presuming you already buy southern-raised queens. Along side your customary practice, start raising your own queens to see if you can do it. Use what you can depend on, but challenge yourself with what will ultimately bring you greater success.

This plan will take the all-or-nothing pressure off your idealized expectations. While your queen-rearing efforts may not deliver immediate results, learning while you still have the means to acquire queens will relieve you of the self-inflicted torture as you struggle to scale the learning curve.

It's like knowing you can always take your cousin to the high school prom while you muster the courage to ask that pretty girl who plays the clarinet in the front row, hoping no one has already asked her as you futilely attempt to orchestrate the perfect opportunity that will never come.

Not that I know anything about taking my cousin to the high school prom.

Unfortunately, when I started raising queens, I made a mental switch, kind of an attitude of "all or none, do it or die." My goal was turning my back on buying mail-order queens, cold turkey, and learning how to raise my own, come hail or high water. No exceptions. No excuses. Anything less was failure.

Such a strident attitude is like fertilizing your frustration and sowing seeds of discontent. I didn't realize my goals were so lofty. I didn't know it would be so flipping hard to master a plastic box. I really thought it would be easier to raise my own queens.

I've often counseled myself, "Try, try again, if at first you don't succeed," but I found myself surrounded by "friends," literally those joyful malcontents who are nothing but Job's comforters. They kept telling me, "Brother, you better quit before you look like a fool. Oops. Too late!"

They thought they were hilarious.

I did not have the success I expected my first year. I swallowed my pride and quietly bought southern queens to meet my needs. The second year started out with disastrous failures larger than my first season.

I was so close to quitting. But the embarrassment of giving up was greater than the humiliation of staying the course until I found success. I was going to learn how to raise queens even if it drove me to strong drink.

I kept telling myself how I would not let this [*expletive deleted*] thing defeat me. I kept repeating "I'm smarter than this [*expletive deleted*] plastic box. I won't give up until they pry it from my cold, dead fingers." But in reality, I hoped victory would come before the situation got this far.

Why is it, when you succeed, they call you, "committed and unwavering," and when you fail, they call you, "obstinate, stubborn, and too stupid to quit?"

Still, I wanted to be the John Cena of queen rearing, who said:

> "I will not quit. I have tasted victory and have been stung by defeat but I WILL NOT QUIT!! I have been knocked down, knocked out, busted up, busted open but I WILL NOT QUIT!! I've often said a man's character is not judged after he celebrates a victory, but by what he does when his back is up against the wall. So no matter how great the set back, how severe the failure, you never give up. You never give

up. You pick yourself up. You brush yourself off. You push forward. You move on. You adapt. You overcome. I haven't backed down from a fight in my life, and I won't start tonight. You can't erase me. I'm gonna make you taste me. My road to [success] starts right now. I won't be stopped. I can't be stopped."

I think anybody can raise queens, but it seems not every one is cut out for it. It does require a level of skill and patience, both which can be learned. But the option of quitting seemed too easy for me, as if I surrendered the battle without even firing my gun. I prefer the option that pushes forward and perseveres all the way to completing Plan A.

Chapter Three:

My Reasons for
Raising My Own Queens

Two of my favorite, national-level speakers at the large conferences and conventions, namely Jennifer Berry, from the University of Georgia, and Gary Reuter, from the University of Minnesota, each share a list of reasons they discovered why beekeepers choose to raise their own queens.

Here are their respective lists, but one thing to keep in mind is this: people may give their reasons, but there's always a reason behind the reason!

Jennifer mentions:
- ✓ To save money,
- ✓ To learn a new skill,
- ✓ To breed for specific traits,
- ✓ Produce a top line of queens,

Gary brings up:

- ✓ To breed for certain traits like,

    --locally adapted stock

    --survivors in your apiaries

- ✓ To not be dependent upon other queen producers (from the south),

- ✓ To save money, though experience is expensive,

- ✓ To have fun, and grasp the intricacies of bee biology,

From my perspective, my personal reasons for raising my own queens, likewise, began with the rather obtuse idea of saving money, but at the heart of saving money was my impatience with buying poorly-mated, mass-produced, inferior queens that likely did not have an adequate egg-laying opportunity in the mating nuc to fully develop their pheromones.

Further, with under developed pheromones, I experienced challenges introducing these mail-order queens to my nucs, and if accepted, many of them just didn't perform to my level of expectation. It wasn't so much *saving* money as much as I was tired of *wasting* money.

And to be fair, not every queen I purchased from a large, commercial queen producer was inferior, but some queens were immediately superseded. Some of them just never got with the program and laid spotty, "shot gun" brood patterns.

Something had to change. That's when I began to ponder the possibilities of raising my own queens. I mean, how hard can it be? And look! Right there in the catalog. There's a non-grafting kit to make raising your own queens even easier! Maybe I should send away for it and get started.

In my early years of beekeeping, the resources to raise your own queens were available, but not easily accessible. We did not yet have the Internet, and many of the resources were written on an academic level. I'm the kind of beekeeper who needs someone to put the cookies on the lower shelf.

Back when I started keeping bees, queen-rearing was just something that didn't catch the interest of most beekeepers. It was easier to get on the phone and mail a check. But this was in an earlier, pre-varroa era and the criteria for queens was considerably simpler. Keeping bees was as simple as throwing those bees in a box and getting out of their way. Honey production was almost guaranteed.

Cavemen were harvesting nice crops of honey. If they could do it, anyone could do it.

So I didn't fight the current. I went with the flow and bought southern-raised, mail-order queens. But I was frustrated with what I was purchasing, but my only viable option close at hand led me to more southern queens.

And that old axiom came true: If you keep buying what you've been buying, you'll keep getting what you've been getting.

I was buying some pretty good queens, on the whole, but it was the handful of mediocre queens that caused me aggravation. With every mediocre queen I received, I lost production. Lost production squandered prime opportunities. Squandered opportunities meant missed revenue. Lost revenue equates to nonexistent profits. I wasted a lot of time, and time is money!

Things changed when more information became available. I found and bought some books, specifically on the topic of how to raise queens. The process seemed pretty straight forward. I had a few questions, namely, is the average beekeepers capable of raising queens? Is there somewhere I can take a class? I was open to expanding my education and adding queen-rearing to my skill set. But raising your own queens was not yet popular enough to tip the scale. All of my beekeeping buddies seemed content to follow the easier path to requeening their hives with southern-raised, mail-order queens.

It was also about this time that varroa mites were making their presence known. Chemical treatments seemed to be short-lived as the varroa quickly developed resistance to our treatments. So I pondered about raising queens from the feral stock, which appeared to thrive in the woods without any kind of treatment.

This idea to use these feral bees to raise replacement queens came after I started using pheromone-baited, swarm traps to catch these feral swarms.

Once I hived the swarms and carried them over to the next season, I perceived some genetic resistance to varroa mites and greater survivability. I must confess these observations were not consistent, and also largely anecdotal from noticing a greater percentage of feral-originated hives surviving my winters.

But the feral swarms fared better than colonies with purchased, mail-order queens. I am also quick to concede I had little experience and still floundered around making a lot of mistakes in my fledgling operation. I really had no clue what I was doing.

Still, I thought I was on to something, though I was only observing the effect without understanding the cause. We know, today, there are many variables for survivability, and without a doubt, varroa has skewed everything we formerly thought to be true.

Colony Collapse Disorder, CCD, has poked us in one eye and we lost our depth perception. The pieces just don't fit the puzzle like they used to and because we are not even sure what the finished puzzle was supposed to look like any more. The times have been challenging and we attempted to evolve and rise to the occasion.

Another reason for raising my own queens was my frustration with ordering mail-order queens, which were subsequently, subjected to the stress of banking (rather than laying eggs in a mating nuc). Banking is the mass storage of queen bees in little cages to ready them for easy access prior to shipping.

I wanted a queen which would have the opportunity to lay eggs in a mating nuc for at least three weeks before she is banked, if she is even banked, at all. Studies have shown the best developed, most sexually mature queens are allowed to lay eggs for three weeks in the mating nuc before being banked. Eventually, the egg laying activity develops her pheromones, which makes for a better introduction and longevity. But banking queens takes a lot of extra equipment.

Despite the revelation from the studies, banking remained the conventional practice of commercial queen producers.

I willingly concede this banking practice is the industry standard, and until someone comes up with a better plan, commercial producers will likely continue this avenue of handling their queens. I felt raising my own queens was a better plan, giving me the advantage to avoid the banking stress. I also had the option of raising ten queens and moving forward by keeping the best four or five.

Additionally, shipping mail-order queens subjects the queen to a variety of temperatures and the subsequent stress while in transit. The shippers (Post Office, UPS, FedEx, the Pony Express, Johnny

Appleseed, Vinny the Dope Smuggler) are increasing reluctant to guarantee live delivery which brings me to my next reason.

My fourth reason for raising my own queens was the disappointment of finding queens that arrived on my door-step, "DOA," that is, "**Dead On Arrival.**"

And with every order of mail-order queens, I observed a mortality rate of about 10% to 25%, on average. Some queen orders came through beautifully; other orders contained nothing but dead bees.

When I called for replacements or refunds, I was typically offered a "credit" on my next order. Some producers asked probing questions as if I was untruthful about receiving dead queens, and I learned to open my order of queens in the presence of the receiving agent (i.e. post office).

Oddly, this option is not something they want you to do inside their building. So we'd step out to my truck and I'd open the package and inspect the queens.

Unfortunately, I don't think the people who work at the post office have any idea what separates a live queen from a dead one, but I'd show them and they'd shake their head as if they knew. Some even gave me an affirming, "Ah, yes." Then they'd hold the queen cage up to the sunlight as if to read the invisible, secret message.

Then there was a mountain of paperwork to fill out, and maybe I'm just frustrated, but it seemed the receiving agent never knew which form to fill out, or what form pertained to honey bees. Queens aren't exactly, "live animals," are they?

No. They're *dead* animals. That's why we're filling out the paperwork.

I can't really blame the producer who has no control over the variables in the shipping process. It has to be maddening to ship such a valuable product, that took so much work to produce, into a heartless system seemingly unconcerned with the contents or how they handle something marked, "fragile," or "keep out of direct sunlight."

Maybe we have a different opinion as to what constitutes "direct" sunlight. Sometimes I am under the opinion that "fragile" is interpreted, "beat the living stuff out of this package and ship it beneath the package of concrete blocks, then travel over bumpy country roads."

I tried insuring my orders, but it took upwards of 90 days to get my money, but the greatest insult to receiving dead bees is I don't have my bees! I lost more time, more opportunities, more production, and more money.

Have I mentioned, "Time is Money?" (Yes!)

The whole shipping industry is evolving, changing every year with respect to guaranteeing (or not guaranteeing) dates of delivery and policies of insuring (or not insuring) live animals. Shipping costs, not surprisingly, continue to rise. But secretly, I'd rather pay the extra money and get a live queen in the mail than scrimp on the cost and have to fight through the forms to get a refund.

I will say, in my former area of Cape Girardeau, Missouri, I have received outstanding cooperation with the local shipping companies who call me the minute the queen shipment arrives at their port or substation.

The managers were always kind and understanding, giving me the option of picking up my package or waiting until the queens took a little joy ride on a scenic route in the back of a delivery truck covering hundreds of hot, dusty miles. With many expressions of gratitude, I picked up the queens at the local substation. The queens didn't seem to resent missing the scenery.

Not surprisingly, prices for queens, like costs of shipping, continue to rise. Not every commercially-raised queen passed the introduction/acceptance test in my apiaries. Requeening a hive or nuc has its own set of tricks and tips. I've paid $25 for a queen only to have the nuc reject her, kill her and basically throw my $25 out the hive entrance.

My fifth reason for raising my own queens was availability. The commercial queen-rearing industry now offers queens pretty much all year long. They continue to produce them, bank them, and then wait for orders.

Some time ago, it was difficult to find a commercial producer who raised mid-summer queens. Mid-summer was my ideal time to split my hives, but I could not find available queens. Many producers were simply sold out and their weather was not conducive to producing good queens. Again, my situation inspired me to ponder my options of raising my own queens so I would have them when I needed them.

My sixth reason is beyond anyone's control. I wrestled with the fickle weather in Missouri and my personal schedule when it came time to introduce those queens for the early splits.

A typical week in in the spring in Missouri is a gorgeous day of 70 degree temperatures followed by six days of 40 degrees with rain and mud. Such weather patterns challenge my hopes of making early splits and introducing mail-order queens.

If I ordered queens and they arrived during a bad weather spell, I'd store the queens, in their cages, in the basement and give each of them a drop of water each day, hoping against hope, that I'd see some better weather.

Maybe I needed to readjust my expectations, but mail-order queens were just not working for me.

To summarize, my reasons for choosing to raise my own queens are:

- ✓ to save money, in essence, to stop wasting money,

- ✓ to raise locally-adapted, survivor stock that better fits my management,
- ✓ to avoid banking and shipping stress,
- ✓ to eliminate wasting time and money on dead queens and lost opportunities,
- ✓ to have queens available when I needed them,
- ✓ to overcome the uncertainties of challenging and unpredictable weather,

So what are your reasons for raising your own queens? Along the way, you may even discover some reasons which may have been previously unknown to you. What was the motivation prompting you to pick up this book? One of my motivations was a desire for good queens. But I didn't want to have to *buy* good queens. I wanted control over the process so I could raise good queens that met my expectations, and have them when I needed them.

In terms of keeping bees sustainably, I want control over the variables. I want to avoid any position of vulnerability depending on vendors and weather which are often not dependable. I want to empower and enable my hopes and dreams and fulfill my purpose. When I articulated my purpose, I fulfilled my vision, and that's when the money started to roll in. Not that beekeeping has to be about the money.

And that's okay.

The NICOT plan I propose in this book is what I found works for me. With a few tweaks here and there to adapt to your local management, it should work for you.

This book will show you the way, step-by-step, to raise your own queens. I don't think you'll find any other resource as detailed as what you hold in your hands, not just on "how" to raise queens with the Nicot system, but "why" these methods work and the reasons I implement the specific steps.

I wish you the greatest success. Remember that success does not require you to look out the window. It only requires you to look in the mirror.

Obviously, you're probably thinking about the end product: an unlimited supply of high-quality queens and the gobs and gobs of money to be saved. It's not the end where success is found; success is found in the beginning.

Here's a little quote I heard:

> *"Why do we set our sights on the finish line, when the most important moment is the start, where we begin to dream, to climb, to soar? There is no finish without the most important part of the day, the start."*

There's more to beekeeping than keeping bees. It's really about you, and your hopes and dreams. You won't finish well, if you don't start well. The most important place to start is with yourself.

I continue to measure myself and my beekeeping expertise with a little old saying about how there are three kinds of people in this world.

> *"There are those who those who make things happen. There are those who watch things happen, and there are those who wonder how things happened and they missed it."*

I want to be in that first group of people and make things happen.

In this demanding process of raising queens, there will be a thousand things to do. My refrain to every song I sing is, *"It's not what I have to do; it's what I want to make happen."*

Thus, the last question ultimately asks, "What do you want to make happen?"

Now go out and make it happen.

Chapter Four:

How Did This Come to Pass?

After finally finding a margin of success with my NICOT queen-rearing kit, I started sharing some of my tips and tricks with other beekeepers. I also disclosed my numerous trials, countless errors, and the many ways in which the NICOT system would not work. Along the way, I discovered I was not the only beekeeper frustrated by this little plastic box. I was asked by a few local bee clubs to share my findings.

Bob Graham, from Dittmer, Missouri, a gracious gentleman and exceptional beekeeper in his own right, heard one of my presentations and asked me to put my process into writing. He referred to it as the "game plan."

Bob also purchased one of these kits, yet wrestled finding the success he hoped would easily come. The

NICOT system offers a seemingly simple alternative to grafting (aka, the Doolittle method) and portrays a perception of convenience, opening the door for anyone desiring to raise their own queens.

I love my NICOT kit, now that I've figured things out, but it possesses several quirks that are not immediately self-evident.

Okay, more than several.

It took me quite a while before I became friends with my NICOT kit. There's a learning curve and a period of acclimation. It's harsh. It's a brutal wake-up call. The procedure is not all butterflies and unicorns, nor is it as undemanding as our imaginations would lead us to believe.

Bob Graham was instrumental in pushing me to put my thoughts on paper. Writing them down, sharing them with him, baring my apicultural soul, and opening it to his critique was hard, but extremely helpful. I owe a great deal of gratitude to Bob.

My Early Struggles

"So how hard can this be?" I boldly reasoned as I ignorantly attempted my first round of queens. It turned out it was harder than I presumed. A lot harder. My mistakes far outnumbered my successes, which wasn't saying much because I didn't have any success my first year.

Zero. As in none.

I forced myself to buy mail-order queens, but until I shared that here, no one knew.

The second season, being too stubborn to quit and too frugal to give up, with the solid resolve to not buy any more mail-order queens, I pressed ahead made adjustments and intuitively diagnosed each step for possible clues as to why I couldn't get this [*expletive deleted*] thing to work. Just how dumb was I?

The process was aggravating and humbling. I was lost. Knowing my wife, she would quickly jump in and tell you I'm the last person on earth to stop and ask for directions when I'm lost. I'm one of those stupid fools who thinks if I repeatedly make the same left hand turn at the stop light, it will somehow, eventually, put me on the right road one of these times.

To my credit, I have stopped and asked for directions, mostly when my wife is not along, but I seem to find the only local fellow who has never ventured beyond the city limits and has no clue what I'm talking about or where it resides.

Thankfully, we now have GPS units, but I find myself arguing with those GPS voices and their advice from time to time. In long run, these voices are usually right. But what I have come to really appreciate is their gentle corrections when I miss the turn these voices have just told me to take. Apparently, there are more ways to get where I want to go and they'll get me there.

For those of us who charge into a project, and fail, we finally read the directions (when provided) and notice something else was still needed. It is my hope that this book fills that void.

The NICOT kit was sufficiently novel that few beekeepers I had really did not know who to ask when it came to my NICOT kit.

Searching the Internet only brought information in bits and pieces. I noticed very small bits and scattered pieces that seldom showed up on the first twenty pages of simple searches with the main search engines. At that time, the NICOT kit was still unfamiliar to a lot of beekeepers, at least those beekeepers who posted in the forums. Youtube had not yet caught on to what it looks like today.

At that time, I swear I was the only beekeeper in Missouri who owned one of these kits as my inquiries directed to my beekeeping buddies received nothing but blank stares, and "What's a NICOT?"

But little by little, my education grew and success honored my diligence and persistence with two queens late in that second season. I did a little better my third season, but I was far from any level of satisfaction, and my results failed to reflect my desires, let alone this magnificent dream of saving money.

Yes, time is money, and at this rate, my time account was overdrawn and I was bouncing proverbial checks all over the place. But little by little, I made more and more progress. I found a few glimpses of success and was able to make a few small deposits against a lot of outstanding checks. But I was still not at the place I wanted to be. That said, I could sense a change in my momentum.

A couple of years down the road, a local beekeeping association invited several beekeepers, including me, to share ideas on queen rearing. I made my NICOT presentation as one possible method of queen rearing that did not require grafting.

The non-grafting aspect was the most attractive feature of the NICOT kit, but this feature greatly overshadowed many of the quirky idiosyncrasies that most people saw as flaws.

I also shared the challenges that tested my beekeeping resolve and nearly undermined my religion, but I offered what I thought was a process that yielded results. Little did I realize I was just barely scratching the surface of how to make this [*expletive deleted*] thing work.

After the presentation, out of the corner of my eye, I caught two wary members from the audience who lurked in the back of the auditorium. On my way out to the parking lot, with a detectable caginess and an air of reticence, they shyly approached me with a whispered request if I might answer a few questions. I really thought they were going to ask me for some money or invite me to participate in a multi-level marketing plan.

With furtive glances to make sure no one was within earshot, they discretely confessed, they, too, purchased a NICOT queen rearing kit, and like me, experienced nothing but frustration and simmering anger at the inventor of such a tortuous device.

I told them I had some rough notes scratched out which I would clean up and send via e-mail. I also told them they were free to e-mail me with questions after reading what I sent.

About a month later, I made a presentation on the NICOT system at a meeting in St. Louis, Missouri. Bob Graham was in the audience that fateful night. That was when he approached me with his request I alluded to earlier.

Thus was born the initial idea of creating this manuscript describing how the NICOT kit works, how it doesn't work, and I make the NICOT kit work for me. Then there is the process by which I raise my own queen honey bees, from cell builders to mating nucs. I wanted to formalize my notes and make my outline presentable.

I kept finding new ways to make this NICOT system work, and work *for* me and work *with* me. The devil, though, was in the details. The dawn was breaking and new light was breaking over the horizon. I felt energized that I was finally getting it.

Bob's request elevated my standards to formalize a manuscript that made sense and filled in some of the missing details. I wanted something I could share with the average beekeeper who wanted to raise queens using the NICOT system. I wanted something I could proudly present, that showed how I conquered the NICOT system, and valiantly subdued this obstinate beast to raise my own superior queens.

Well, okay. That last statement is a bit much.

But I owe a great debt of gratitude to Bob. Without his friendly reminders, I doubt I possessed the enduring motivation to put this little manuscript together and revise it for public perusal. I might have given up, not just on this manuscript, but giving up on the NICOT method, itself.

I continued refining my practices, honing my techniques, providing fresh content and additional material to my rough draft. More material required further revision and I modified, corrected and improved the written manuscript further through 2010.

Without a doubt, there is a wealth of information all around us and I hope this manuscript brings you closer to your goals and objectives with respect to raising your own queens. Sometimes all you have to do is ask the right questions, then patiently allow Providence to bring you the right people, at the right time, possessing the right answers and the available resources.

It amazes me the depth of experience and the collective wisdom that goes untapped at bee meetings until that fateful, serendipitous moment, at the most unlikely time, when someone says, "I got a question..."

Most times I learn more over lunch or in the casual conversations in the hallways as opposed to listening to the main speaker in the large auditorium. I have also learned to hold back my opinions and just listen to what others are doing. You can learn a lot just by being quiet. Everyone doesn't have to listen to everything you know.

Another Caveat

Let me warn you. What you have before you is still a "work in progress." During the summer of 2012, just when I thought I was ready to announce to the world how I had reached my level of success, I was humbled. I learned some more things on top of more things. I don't think anyone ever reaches that point of knowing everything and I stand amazed at how much knowledge, wisdom and experience, not to mention patience and perseverance, it takes to successfully raise honey bees.

Or lots of luck…or maybe it's all of these things.

Thankfully, the bees are rather independent, little bugs and fend for themselves despite my ignorance and well-intentioned stupidity, not to mention, my procrastination. And you wonder why I'm so impatient with people who procrastinate? I have first-hand experience how devastating it can be to say, "Oh, maybe not today. I'll catch up tomorrow…"

This manuscript, updated for 2014, further revised in 2019, continues my journey and presents my most recent account how I refined and revised my process. In its present form, this stuff works, but no doubt it can stand improving. Very likely, I'll learn more things next summer to refine my process. Beekeeping is a perpetual, educational journey with no final destination of reaching perfection. Success is a moving target. Thankfully, even a blind sow will root up an acorn once in a while.

Having kept bees since 1981, I find I'm still learning a lot every year as each season throws the beekeeping community a new curve, a new parasite, a new pesticide. I still remember, fondly, the pre-varroa years. I think the most fortunate beekeepers are those who started keeping bees after varroa arrived and are not handicapped by this wistfully idiotic longing for the ease of those good old days.

Common wisdom suggests when the student is ready, the teacher appears. My bees continue filling the role as my greatest teacher, though their student is often not ready and, too often, requires remedial instruction. I continue that idealistic fantasy that someday I'll figure it out. I'm sure my bees share this hope, as well.

In the pages that follow, I line out the details of my method using the NICOT kit the way it works for me. Obviously, you'll need to adjust and modify the particulars to fit your specific region and suit the unique ways you keep bees.

Greg Hannaford of Tulsa, Oklahoma, inspires me with his reminder, "The principles are the same but the methods will undoubtedly vary."

This manuscript is how I do it, or in many of the beekeeping circles we'd call this a "HIDI talk," (**H**ow **I D**o **It**).

Still, the principles I've presented, as they pertain to the NICOT system of raising queens, remain the same while you evaluate and modify my methods of "how I do it" to your particular area and your specific goals and aspirations.

What you have at your fingertips (or in front of you on your screen as a download) will give you a good start. I don't claim to have all the answers, but use my information as I present it. Learn from me. Ponder why I choose to do it this way. Debate my methods. Feel free to argue my conclusions.

Then take your circumstances into account and improve upon my process. The NICOT system works for me, and this book describes *how* I make it work.

I invite you to refine and revise it in order to make it work for you. I offer my encouragement to adjust it in any way you see fit. You're even invited to tell me I have it all wrong.

And at the end of this book, you'll find my e-mail address. I will gladly answer any question that might arise. Remember, too, this is not the last word. Maybe you have a better idea for future revisions. We can all learn from each other.

Build a Foundation of Information

I would be remiss not to mention there are a hundred different ways to raise queens, many of which do not involve grafting. All of them are valid. All of them work, more or less, though you'll find some of these methods more advantageous for you in your circumstances. We're all inclined to different approaches which is one the beautiful aspects about keeping honey bees. Beekeeping is a journey of many roads.

I stumbled upon this NICOT system and it "clicked" with me for some reason, perhaps because it sounded like the Doolittle method for lazy beekeepers.

For starters, if you have not already done so, I recommend reading and/or running an Internet search on queen-rearing. You'll discover multiple links to an embarrassing abundance of material. Many times, the quantity of information simply overwhelms my sensibilities. Much of it is redundant.

Still, I sift through a lot of chaff searching for kernels of wheat. The wheat is there for those who search and don't have kids needing the computer to check their e-mail or update their Facebook page.

My kids, now adults, have graduated to "smart" phones with expensive data plans and they do most of their online stuff from the convenience of their left hand. I still seem to work by the seat of my pants.

The good news is every method shares the same, ultimate goal of producing queens, irrespective of which journey one takes to reach the destination. The commonality of the various methods draws together the essence of queen-rearing and begins building the foundation to understanding the assumptions behind the NICOT method.

The Internet also presents a plethora of good information on basic queen bee biology which is the cornerstone to any method on raising queens.

In searching the Internet, keep this truth in mind: There is no one, single, "right" way to raise queens, other than the way that works for you. Everyone will do it differently, and many different methods may even seem to contradict the others.

I humbly offer my non-grafting approach as what works for me. I have full confidence it will work for you. If it doesn't work or you absolutely detest the NICOT method, find someone you don't like. Give them your NICOT kit and this book as your gift. Smile as you hand it over to them. They'll thank you and call you a "champ."

Call it poetic justice or sweet revenge, however those chips may fall.

Knowledge is Power

To paraphrase a quote by Mark Twain, the beekeeper who can read but does not is no better off than the illiterate beekeeper who cannot read.

Additionally, I paraphrase an old proverb which suggests, "The average beekeeper only reads one book a year—that's why they're an average beekeeper."

Knowledge is power. If you really want to raise your own queens, and do it well, get your hands on every book you can find on this subject, but I'll warn you, there are not that many books.

It also helps to read those first chapters on basic honey bee biology that seem to find their way into every book on beginning beekeeping. These are the chapters I always skipped because I wanted to get to the good stuff like how to shake package bees into a newly constructed hive.

I would strongly advocate acquiring copies of the standard queen-rearing books. A search of any on-line retail books seller (i.e., www.amazon.com) will yield a number of options to include a plethora of used copies, many which are out of print.

I occasionally troll through www.eBay.com for older books, though few bargains exist here. The ebay experience leaves me wondering about the legitimacy of the bidding process, but that's another rant for another day.

Consult any current beekeeping supply catalog for the latest offerings. The best books are constantly being republished. Some of these books are intense and technical, but knowledge is power and you need all the knowledge you can get your hands on.

I bypass my local public library. They only carry, out of necessity, what appeals to the general public. Their funds are limited. I would encourage you to donate a few NEW books on beekeeping to help them out.

In my personal beekeeping library I possess,

- ✓ *Rearing Queen Honey Bees* by Roger A. Morse (Wicwas Press, 1994),

- ✓ *Contemporary Queen Rearing* by Harry H. Laidlaw, Jr. (Dadant Publication, 1979), and

- ✓ *Queen Rearing* by Harry H. Laidlaw, Jr. and J. E. Eckert (University of California Press, 1962).

I count these classic books among the "oldies but goodies." They are quite technical and thorough, and present foundational and conventional standards for understanding the biology of raising queen honey bees.

I also have copies of:

- ✓ *Better Queens* by Jay Smith (1949),

- ✓ *Increase Essentials* by Lawrence John Connor (Wicwas Press, 2006),

- ✓ *Breeding Super Bees* by Steve Tabor (A.I. Root, 1987),

✓ *Queen Rearing* by L. E. Snellgrove (1946),

✓ *Queen Rearing Simplified* by Vince Cook (1986),

✓ *Practical Queen Rearing* by Charles and Pauline Dublon, and a book by my favorite author,

✓ Frank Pellet, *Practical Queen Rearing* (published by the American Bee Journal, 1918, Third Edition).

Some of these books are dated, but queen rearing is a timeless art. The basics haven't changed, but certainly the issues of varroa mites and other current problems like sub-lethal residues of miticides bring new challenges to the table.

On my "wish list" of books I hope to acquire soon to round out my collection, I'm looking at:

✓ *Queen Bee: Biology, Rearing and Breeding* by David R. Woodward (2010),

✓ *Queen Rearing Essentials* by Lawrence John Connor (Wicwas Press, 2009),

✓ *Bee Sex Essentials*, by Lawrence John Connor (Wicwas Press),

- ✓ *Scientific Queen-Rearing*, by G. M. Doolittle (Wicwas Press),

- ✓ *Increase Essentials* (updated) by Lawrence John Connor (Wicwas Press),

- ✓ *A Year's Work in the Out Apiary* (Reprinted) by G. M. Dolittle (Wicwas Press).

And as a side note, I used to own many of Larry Connor's books. He's an excellent writer, a gentleman and a scholar, and a crackerjack beekeeper. I enthusiastically "loaned" his books out to new beekeepers, and some them have yet to find their way back home to my shelves.

Chapter Five:

The Tools You'll Need

To Get Started

In my method of raising queen honey bees, I use a "Complete Queen Rearing Kit" sold by **Mann Lake Beekeeping Supply** (www.mannlakeltd.com), as well as **Betterbee, Inc.** (www.betterbee.com). Sometimes suppliers list this kit under the branded names of "NICOT" or "Cupularve" and sometimes generically and innocuously listed simply as a "queen-rearing kit."

The complete kit costs around $80 and contains everything necessary to raise two or three dozen queens. You'll need a couple of groove-top/groove bottom, medium frames to assemble the parts. Annual replacement supplies cost around $10 per season after you raise your initial crop of queens. Extra components are available if you want to expand the number of queens you produce.

At one time, Mann Lake was the exclusive supplier carrying this kit in their catalog, and thus many beekeepers mistakenly bestow upon it the name, "Mann Lake Queen Rearing Kit," as I often do, myself.

Other suppliers are adding the NICOT kit to their catalogs, which I believe is due to the growing interest in raising local queens, and also because of the reluctance of hobby beekeepers to embrace the practice of grafting larvae. These two reasons fit my interest in raising my own queens.

If you regard the initial cost of the kit as expensive, I challenge you to stop and consider the number of queens you can buy for that same price.

Not very many.

When I looked at the price of my NICOT kit, I thought it was kind of pricey. Then I thought of the availability and quality of the mail-order queens I was purchasing. I thought I could do better. I also started thinking about the control I desired in choosing which qualities I wanted in the locally-adapted genetics in my queens. The NICOT kit gave me the opportunity to raise new queens from the best of the best hives in my apiaries.

In my opinion, my purchase of the NICOT queen rearing kit was the best investment I ever made with respect to my beekeeping future.

There are other systems (Jenter is similar, Dadant has the EZI queen system) and more and more supply catalogs are carrying similar units plus offering the conventional tools of the trade like Chinese grafting tools and the JZ-BZ line of queen-rearing supplies.

You will find there are vast similarities between the NICOT system and others kits, and basic queen biology does not change with the purchase of a kit. While I haven't tried other non-grafting kits sold in the catalogs, no doubt some of the NICOT's tricks and tips enlighten the process offered by the other kits.

An Alternative to the Conventional Methods

My express purpose in this book explains the NICOT queen-rearing system and how the average beekeeper implements its unique design and overcomes the distinctive hurdles to raising queens without grafting. The NICOT system is not the only non-grafting approach, but it works for me.

And thanks to the Internet (www.youtube.com in particular) beekeepers find access to an excess of resources demonstrating queen-raising techniques. There are many and varied approaches to raising queens.

The majority of the methods mention a practice of physically and manually, lifting and transferring early-stage larvae from a cell in the comb to a series of cups on a top bar, a process called, "grafting." Grafting, sometimes referred to as the Doolittle method, is the industry convention.

If you pressed me, I would hazard a guess that 90% of all beekeepers who raise queens do so by grafting larvae. I often wonder how many potential queen raisers tried grafting, then gave up because it's tricky and it took a steady hand, with good lighting, and sharp eyesight. Too often, I randomly possess only two of those three requisite skills. Sharp eyesight is becoming a forgone ability, in my case.

Most beekeeping schools, in their classes teaching the art and craft of queen-rearing, utilize grafting as their core method. Most initial attempts at grafting are not immediately met with success, and in our world of instant microwave results, immediate e-mail communication and spontaneous texting, successful grafting becomes the main hurdle for many potential queen producers. It's not something learned by accident, nor is it something we do every day like brushing our teeth.

The old axiom, "Practice makes perfect," is great encouragement for many endeavors, more than rightly applying to grafting, but frustration is the typical, initial outcome of learning how to graft for the first time.

Patience, I am told, is the key to learning how to graft. That and a comb loaded with hundreds of newly hatched larvae so you can practice, and practice, and practice without concern for how many larvae it takes in the process of practicing and getting everything down pat.

Unfortunately, just the idea of grafting intimidates a large percentage of beekeepers and dims their hopes of ever raising their own queens.

They buy into the idea that grafting is the only way to raise queens, and with the predominance of classes only teaching the grafting method, beginners believe they have no alternative choice but to learn to graft. Regretfully, feeling grafting is impossible for their skill level, they opt to purchase their replacement queens like we've done for a hundred years.

And don't get me wrong, there is nothing principally wrong with buying your queens from a commercial queen producer. I simply approach this process of queen-rearing from the perspective of raising locally-adapted queens, suited to your area under your management, as more advantageous and a step in the direction of sustainable beekeeping.

The benchmark of queen-rearing is grafting, the mandatory technique that winnows out the potentials from the professionals. I won't argue against grafting even though I don't practice this method, but I firmly believe alternative queen-rearing methods offer equally satisfactory options with similarly acceptable results.

With the NICOT system, anyone can raise their own queens and not worry about grafting, or even losing any sleep over wondering how they could possibly go about learning how to graft.

SPOILER ALERT!: I don't graft. I never wanted to graft. I never even wanted to learn how to graft despite a hundred queen breeders telling me to quit my sniveling, grab that grafting tool, "man up" and graft. They continually harp on me how the gold standard of queen rearing is the Doolittle method of grafting larvae. I have been told on numerous occasions that I need to "get with the program" and learn how to graft.

Despite their threats and derisive insults, I don't graft. I don't see the need for even learning how to graft. My esteem as a beekeeper is not tied to my ability to graft. But I do respect their enthusiasm.

One of the benefits of the NICOT system is taking the guess work out of estimating the age of the larvae to be transferred. With grafting, one must also learn what young larvae looks like, discerning which larvae are too old. The NICOT offers a simple approach based on finding newly hatched larvae.

One leading beekeeper from Vermont disdainfully describes the NICOT kit as "that plastic contraption." I detect a subtle good-natured recrimination of "guilt by association," backhandedly criticizing those of us who opt for this method.

Nevertheless, the NICOT system works for me. If you want to learn how to graft, please don't let me be a wet blanket and quench your spirit. Go for it. Make it work for you. Many successful grafters tell me it's easier than what first appears and I should give it a serious attempt.

But if you're like me, chairman of the crowd of namby-pamby, weak-willed non-grafters, these plastic contraptions work. I think using the NICOT kit is so slick, it's almost like cheating. But I'll warn you, there are some drawbacks. There are some tricks and some absolute prerequisites you'll have to execute or you'll end up with nothing but frustration.

That's why I wrote this book. I share the little details how these plastic contraptions work, along with the inside secrets I learned which eliminate the frustration and minimize the profanity. I also mention some of the obligatory nuances I learned along the way.

You are still free to sign up for grafting classes, and thankfully, with the growing interest in small-scale queen-rearing, more and more local associations are teaching the grafting craft.

As for me and my house, we use NICOT. The NICOT system helps those of us who are too stubborn and perhaps too short-sighted, ignorant or just too ornery to learn how to graft larvae and raise queens with the Doolittle method.

Go with what works for you. Remember what I said earlier: There is no "right" method except the method that works for you.

Chapter Six:
Queen Rearing Fundamentals

There are some basic truths to queen-rearing that apply to everyone regardless of your method to raise queens.

First, a quick primer on queen biology. (Grab a real book on queen-rearing if you want all the gory details.) Here is some basic information that's just enough to get you through the gate.

The development of a normal worker egg covers 21 days to reach maturity, and upon maturity, this bee emerges as an ordinary worker bee. The worker starts out as a fertilized egg, which contrasts with a drone that originates from an unfertilized egg. Both will go through the four common stages of egg, larva, pupa, and emergence as an adult. Drones take longer to mature and will emerge at 24 days.

Every queen bee starts out as a worker egg, which is a surprising fact to most beginners who ask, "Where do queen honey bees come from?" An adult worker bee is merely an under-developed queen honey bee. Or looking at it another way, the queen bee is a fully matured worker.

An adult worker will never become a queen, though oddly they have the ability to lay unfertilized eggs which are destined to become drones. You'll often hear of colonies headed by laying workers when the normal pheromones holding the colony in balance are skewed out of proportion.

When a queen honey bee lays a fertilized egg, the egg requires three-and-a-half days to hatch. Upon hatching, the young nurse bees in the colony feed royal jelly to all the newly hatched larvae. All larvae receive royal jelly in their early stages of development, even the larvae destined to remain as workers.

But in an environment lacking a queen, young nurse bees flood some of the larvae with royal jelly for the duration of their entire larval stage, then rework, remodel, and enlarge the normal-sized worker cells into functional queen-sized cells. The larvae destined to remain as workers are switched over to a mixture of pollen and nectar often referred to as "bee bread."

The nurse bees feed copious amounts of royal jelly to the larvae destined to become queens for a period of time significantly longer than they would to a normal worker larva. This abundantly fed larva now matures into a queen bee.

The extended feeding of royal jelly makes all the difference how a normal worker larva matures into the advanced developmental stages and becomes a queen. As I alluded to earlier, a queen is a "completed" worker bee, thanks to the wonder-working power of royal jelly. Conversely, a worker bee is a queen bee whose development was arrested and halted because it was weaned from an unlimited supply of royal jelly.

A point to remember is how both the worker and the queen start out with the same beginnings as a fertilized egg. Without extraordinary intervention, the fertilized egg becomes a worker. The larva destined to become a queen receives the preferential treatment of unlimited royal jelly and her cell is remodeled to accommodate her extra growth.

When I talk to non-beekeepers, using human anatomy as an analogy, I often explain a worker bee is a female that has not yet reached puberty, and never will. Because her larval diet of nectar and pollen (lacking unlimited royal jelly) restricts her development, this worker bee never matures to the point where she mates and lays eggs. Yes, there are exceptions with "laying workers."

I also draw the analogy that a queen bee is a female that has gone through puberty. And thanks to her diet of royal jelly, she matures to the point where she possesses the ability and the opportunity to mate and lay eggs.

Diet and nutrition make all the difference between an ordinary worker bee and a sexually-mature queen bee. But these larvae chosen to become potential queens also require healthy, well-fed young nurse bees in the cell builder colony to produce the royal jelly. An abundance of young nurse bees needed to feed the developing larvae is likewise the difference between average queens and highly productive queens. Nutrition is paramount!

Because nutrition is a key component in a queen's development, you can begin to appreciate how merely taking two frames of open brood, with the attached nurse bees, and placing them in a nuc box, forcing the construction of "emergency" queen cells, is not the optimal method of raising your own queens. Despite the fact that half of the people in any given bee club will raise their hand and confess to using this method, the common sense logistics and academic research will tell you high-quality queens are just not possible with this two-frame method.

But there's always someone in every bee club that will tell you this method works "just fine." Okay. If they're satisfied with those queens, and the productivity and longevity suit them, who am I to argue?

Nutrition is very important, as is the number of worker bees providing the nutrients to the developing larvae. This means a good cell builder colony (the queenless colony you create to build the queen cells) needs to be populated with large numbers of healthy, young, nurse bees.

These young nurse bees that feed the larvae also need a high plain of nutrition themselves to produce the royal jelly. This importance plays out when we put together our cell builder colonies, but I'm getting ahead of myself.

The worker egg requires three-and-a-half days to hatch. The larval stage for both workers and queens is five-to-six days. A normal worker receives royal jelly for two or three of those six days. Yet a worker destined to mature into a queen will have royal jelly fed to her for all six days, and when the potential queen larva is sealed up into the pupa stage, she is literally swimming in royal jelly.

Again, this extended feeding of the royal jelly accelerates the growth and development of that worker larva and forever changes her destiny to that of a queen bee.

Without the diet of royal jelly, the larva will only remain an ordinary worker bee. I also cannot help but repeat myself how the quality of the feeding requires an overabundance of healthy, well fed, young nurse bees in the cell builder colony. In a later chapter in this book, I'll detail setting up this cell builder colony, and insuring the presence of young nurse bees that convert newly hatched larvae into queens.

The pupa stage for a worker bee runs ten to eleven days, where the rapidly developing queen only takes six days. In the end, the worker takes a total of 21 days from egg to emergence; the queen emerges 16 days from the day her egg is laid.

Here are five key points to remember.

> All queen bees start out as worker eggs.

> Royal jelly makes the difference when fed to the larva.

> Royal jelly is produced by the young nurse bees in the colony.

> Their ability to produce royal jelly is dependent upon the health and nutrition of the colony. They are the bees that feed the bees.

> It takes a large population of healthy nurse bees to produce the large quantity of royal jelly that is required to produce high-quality queens.

Well-fed cell builder colonies produce robust nurse bees which, in turn, produce superior queens. Choosing which colonies you'll use as the cell builder colonies is also important.

I raise all this biological information bringing up the next vital component to raising high-quality queens: converting age-appropriate larvae. The younger the larvae chosen, the better the emerging queen.

All experienced queen producers, irrespective of their method of moving/transferring larvae to a cell builder colony, know selecting the youngest, newly hatched larva works to their advantage.

As soon as possible, the earlier one can catch the larva in its development, means more royal jelly is fed for a longer duration and the nurse bees produce a better queen. There is a critical window of opportunity to move larvae from a queen-right hive to the queen-less cell builder colony that cannot be ignored.

For this reason, you often hear of queen producers grafting larvae when they are 12- to 24-hours old. You might stretch this window to 36 hours, but most optimally, the earlier the better.

Under the normal conventions of the Doolittle method of manually transferring (grafting) larvae from the queenright colony to the queenless cell builder requires the beekeeper to know and identify which larvae are the youngest.

SPOILER ALERT!: The NICOT system makes this identification and decision foolproof. But I'm getting ahead of myself.

The concept here is the analogy of "switching tracks." When a fertilized egg is laid, under normal circumstances, it is riding on the normal worker bee track. To convert it into a high-quality queen, the queen producer needs to switch it to the queen track, as soon as possible in its larval development. Hence, the desire of commercial queen producers to graft larvae is in their 12- to 24-hour stage of life.

The trick of switching these tracks, or switching larvae from worker mode to queen mode, happens when we transfer the newly hatched larvae into a broodless, queenless environment, which for us, is our cell builder colony.

Having no queen in this cell builder colony, and no other larvae available to make a queen, the young nurse bees jump on our transferred larvae and make queen cells. The nurse bees pull the switch on changing tracks by feeding bountiful amounts of royal jelly.

The Temptation of a Futile Option:

This discussion regarding the crucial window for producing favorable queens raises a question on the subject of transferring eggs. Many of us NICOT users ponder the alternative of transferring eggs instead of waiting and trying to catching 12- to 24-hour old larvae, even 36-hour old larvae.

How much easier it would be to transfer eggs! We would be freed from the tyranny of the schedule! When the eggs hatch, the nurse bees in the cell builder stand ready to jump on the larvae right away upon hatching for the highest possible quality queens. Our worries are over; our problems are solved!

Stop. Put the cork back in the Champaign bottle. It doesn't work this way. For some unknown reason, transferring eggs in the NICOT method is unacceptable to the bees. The nurse bees cannibalize the eggs or they wave their magic antennae and make the eggs disappear. Transferring newly hatched larvae, as young as you can catch them, is the only option when using the NICOT queen-rearing kit. Forget about transferring eggs.

Should you suffer from short-term memory loss, don't worry. The futility of transferring eggs arises in future chapters as a reminder. And if you still fail to heed my warnings and mistakenly transfer eggs, the bees will gently reward you with a vacant cell cup as a reminder.

When I've tried transferring eggs and the cell builder rejected my attempts, the vacant cell cup was like a slap in the face. It's up to you to choose which expletives fit the situation. Or you can simply say, "Yep, Grant. You were right."

But don't say I didn't warn you. Don't try and transfer eggs. Don't even entertain the idea.

Seasonal Cues:

The best time to raise queen cells is during a time when the field bees bring ample pollen and nectar into the hives. Pollen and nectar is food for the young nurse bees that feed the developing larvae. We want to "feed the bees (nurse bees) that feed the bees (larvae)."

The best time to breed/mate queens is when the weather has moderated, such as in May and June. This is what worked in my former bee yards in southeast Missouri. This is also swarm season when the bees are amped up to raise queens because the weather is suitable and promising. This is the time of year when drones are plentiful and the weather is suited for flying.

Rookie queen producers often forget the second half of a successfully mated, productive queen is ample drones, the "studs" of the apiary, though technically, drones are nothing but parasites in a matriarchal society. Their sole purpose in life is to have sex with a new queen.

Another key to producing quality queens is working with the colony's desires and inclinations. May and June are optimal months when the bees appear willing to collaborate with my efforts of raising queens. Weather and availability of forage elevate the colony's level of cooperation. Everybody is happy and content, falling all over themselves to accommodate my plans. Raising queens this time of year also gives me a long window to evaluate the queens and kick out the sub-par performers.

I've raised queens in May, June, July, and even in August. Without question, I produce my best queens in May and June. My percentage of queens I successfully raise in July and August drops dramatically, likely due to the nectar dearth we normally suffer. It's as if the bees know it's an inopportune time to raise new queens. The lack of forage makes everyone jumpy and suspicious. Robbing is on the increase.

The swarm season in southeast Missouri wraps up in early July and I always use the 4th of July as my benchmark, though every year is different. I have found myself musing, "This is a very unusual summer we're having." Then I remember I said the same thing the year before, and the year before that year. It's like we have no "normal" anymore.

Raising queens after the swarming season raises the colony's sense of resistance as if they're fighting against my efforts. They're trying to tell me it's not the best time to be raising queens if the nectar and pollen supplies have dried up.

Several speakers at many of the conferences agree; successful beekeepers listen to what the bees are communicating. The bees are always trying to tell us what's happening in their little lives, if we would but listen and pay attention when we open the hives.

Many times, a simple observation at the entrance gives a host of clues as to how well the bees are working, or not working. Even during a nectar dearth, bees still go out and forage, but the pickings are slim. This usually prompts most queens to begin shutting down. The mood in the colony shifts.

It's not impossible to raise late season queens, but I experience better success earlier in the season. If you're new to queen-rearing, I'd highly recommend making your attempts when the bees are the most congenial toward helping you, after all, the bees really do all the work. You can, at least, accommodate their willingness. After all, the bees really do the work. You have to work with them.

If you are old enough to remember an old commercial on television, Mother Nature samples a brand-name margarine and replies, "Why, that's my wonderful, creamy butter."

The voice-over announcer corrects Mother Nature, that what she holds in her hand is not her creamy butter but a substitute made from soybean oil. She scowls and wags her finger in disappointment, replying, "It's not nice to fool Mother Nature." Then she conjures up an instant thunderstorm.

I sometimes wonder if my efforts and attempts of raising queens in July and August isn't working against, even attempting to fool Mother Nature, and doing nothing but raising her ire. It just seems like raising late season queens is like twisting arms, uh, legs forcing the bees to cooperate. Am I even trying to fool myself that it doesn't matter when I attempt to raise queens?

The ultimate key to queen quality is the availability of drones. The definitive benchmark of my success is found when the queen settles down after her mating flight and begins producing solid patterns of brood. No matter how carefully I watch the details or pay attention to the schedule, if I don't have plenty of drones to finish the process, all my work is for naught. It also helps to have nice, calm weather for these mating flights.

Unfortunately, drones are thought to be little more than the icing on the cake, but in reality, they are the roof that completes a house. If you have a poor roof, you're going to suffer from the exposure to the elements. Drones contribute 50% of the genetics to those future workers, but we treat them as accessories.

On the other end of the season, early queen-rearing, i.e., April, thought to be a necessity in the traditional, dominant model of commercial beekeeping, governs many of our current management options. Even the hobbyist and back yard beekeepers willingly drink up this Koo-aid®.

But drones are not in abundance and the weather is not cooperative for mating flights.

I've acquiesced to focusing my queen-rearing efforts to May and June. There is just no way I am able to raise queens early enough in April to make my spring splits, and July and August have low percentages of success that I wonder if it's even worth my effort.

It surprises me how many beekeeping classes for beginners base the teaching on the dominant model of beekeeping. We expect the beginner and hobbyist to operate under the compulsory expectation of a commercial production model and inform them we need early season queens in order to split our hives.

The fact remains, that in southeast Missouri, we could not raise locally-sourced queens early enough for spring splits under the dominant beekeeping model.

To have a mated queen ready to go in mid-April requires us to start the process roughly 28 days earlier, and our fickle spring weather presents a huge challenge to this endeavor. Drones are not usually plentiful this early in the season, either.

Those of us who want to make early season splits resign ourselves to buying southern-raised queens. Don't get me wrong. This method works, more or less, and a lot of beekeepers subscribe to this dominant model of beekeeping and they're quite happy with it.

Splitting Hives

The dominant model works, and works well if you purchase southern-raised, mail-order queens, but things are changing. The traditional way of splitting hives is a good method of making increase and retarding swarming, no question.

"Making increase" is the term we use to describe how we refill our winter dead-outs, and splitting hives is a good management tool to keep your colonies from swarming.

Swarming is something most modern beekeepers seek to avoid as it weakens the hive and greatly diminishes the potential honey crop. I've always viewed splits as an artificial swarm, but the good news is the swarm doesn't get away and you don't have to climb a forty-foot tree to retrieve them. Simply put, splitting works to prevent swarming and it's not a complicated procedure.

Personally, I produce honey so I'm not enthralled with the idea of early-season splitting. I work diligently to retard the swarming by other means, and to pull this off, one must be diligent.

Traditional beekeepers who subscribe to the dominant paradigm often press me and ask, "Why work so hard when splitting works?"

I don't argue that it doesn't work, but my point is splitting a colony will the amount of honey I can harvest. My experience shows, even as I split a colony into two units, their combined honey harvest will not equal the honey I can harvest from a single colony that I didn't split. But this greater amount of honey comes from an unsplit colony only happens when that colony does not swarm.

One, unswarmed hive far out-produces the combined honey harvest of the two split hives. And I can point you to research from Walter Gojmerac (University of Wisconsin) to back up this claim.

But on the other hand, if you can't control swarming, then your honey production is going to falter.

It gets back to a message I preach over and over about how one's purpose for keeping bees governs the management practices and how seriously one takes their profession, even if it is "just a hobby."

My wife calls my obsession with honey bees, "a hobby on steroids." The fruit of my commitment and passion (two other words found in my apicultural sermons) manifests itself in the abundance of my honey harvest.

Some beekeepers measure my success, then incredulously complain, "You're the luckiest guy I know."

Ah, but what is "luck" other than preparations made to intercept opportunity?

But that's another sermon for another day. It's time for me to get off my soapbox. You'll find a continuation of this rant in my book on sustainable practices, **"Sustainable Beekeeping: Surviving in an Age of CCD,"** available on Amazon.com.

Or check out another resource, **"A Ton of Honey: Managing Your Hives for Maximum Production,"** also on Amazon.com.

Exercising my options

So instead of opting for southern-raised queens and acquiescing to the traditional industry standard and the dominant paradigm of making splits in the early spring, I started looking for a different system. I continued to search for alternative methods (other than splitting) to prevent swarming.

I looked into raising my own queens from my own, locally-adapted stock. Of course, I had to wait until the weather moderated. This meant I could no longer buy into the commercial, conventional paradigm of early spring splits.

Also, I still had that stubbornly obstinate hang-up about being forced to graft. I ran across the NICOT kit in a Mann Lake beekeeping supply catalog and thought it looked easier than learning how to graft.

What I really learned is "looks" can be deceiving. While the NICOT system is easier to navigate, it still has its special features and idiosyncrasies that need to be honored and respected or you'll come up empty. Honoring and respecting these features was part of my lengthy education in learning how to make the NICOT system work for me.

So here's how my honey production system evolved. Each spring, I manipulate my hives to prevent swarming. I build up large colonies and put my supers on the hives early. Our nectar flow begins with a teasing trickle in late April, but really kicks in with a furious flow around Mother's Day. Then it's over in a blink of an eye by the 4th of July.

That's in a normal year, but the only place I find "normal" is on the washing machine in the basement. And in reality, there is no reality. A "regular" day depends on my consumption of bran cereal that morning.

So in the middle of May, after I get everything supered up for the honey flow and I have a moment to catch my breath, I start raising my queens and set up small mating nucs. I raise a crop of queens around the first of June. In July, I harvest my honey and split my hives to build up for the next year and requeen the splits with my queens from the mating nucs.

Bear in mind, and I'll mention this later, not every queen cell in every mating nuc results in a mated queen. Not every cell hatches. Not every emerged queen finds her way back from her mating flight.

Once the queen starts laying, not every queen will meet my level of expectation.

It's a game of percentages working with diminishing returns, so more equipment is needed and more patience is required as you raise your own queens.

When you buy a mail-order queen, the queen producer has already absorbed all of these attritions that lead up to the final product, a mated queen. When raising your own queens, the attrition rate is just something that will have to be figured into your calculations for the desired outcome.

My little rule of thumb, based on my experiences, is that you'll need to start out raising twice as many queens as you'll think you'll need at the end of the process.

In raising your own handful of queens, you begin developing a respect and a reverence for the commercial queen breeders who raise tens of thousands of queens and whom we so casually malign for the lack of quality and their inability to meet our impatient demands when we suddenly require a single queen overnight. Some days, it's a wonder they even take our phone calls.

Queen-rearing isn't hard, but it is work and takes time and energy, along with a focused effort. More and more beekeeping clubs are promoting locally-adapted queen-rearing initiatives and offering classes to learn how to graft. I applaud the efforts in teaching beginners how to graft, but if any club offers me a scholarship, I suggest passing it along to someone who wants to learn how to graft and appreciates the process more than me.

I want to keep hives strong going into a honey flow so I don't normally split my colonies, but I do need to do something regarding swarming. I find splitting my hives in the early spring weakens the colony and reduces my honey crop...not as bad as swarming, but splitting a hive still weakens it.

So my goal is to use other methods of swarm control. I like Walt Wright's "checkerboarding" strategies and Lloyd Sechrist's "expanding brood nest" technique.

Both of these practices maintain the integrity of the hive allowing the population to grow without triggering the swarming impulse. Both of these practices work, provided I do the work.

These management options allow me to harvest an abundant honey crop, more than if I split my hives in the early part of the season. Once the supers come off the hives, any honey production during the rest of the summer is marginal. This is a good time to make splits, however, I have my queens ready to go and laying in my mating nucs.

So I gave up the notion of making early spring splits with mail-order queens from southern queen producers. Buying southern queens is fraught with complications, anyway, so I opt to raise my own queens in late May and early June and split my hives after the honey harvest in July.

Genetics vs. Nutrition:

The work of C. L. Farrar suggests raising queens in times of abundant nectar and pollen, even if they were from average genetic stock, were superior to queens of exceptional genetic stock raised under a shortage of nectar and pollen (such as, early in the spring when the weather is fickle). This information validated my desire to raise queens in May and June in my former area of southeast Missouri.

I also made mention of this idea earlier when I said it takes an abundance of well-fed, young nurse bees to feed the larvae. Young nurse bees derive their nutrition from incoming nectar and pollen. Populations of young nurse bees come from queens who lay a lot of eggs, and the time when queens are in this go-go-go mood to lay eggs is in the early spring when nectar and pollen are abundant.

Can you begin to see how a many of these factors are related and all fit into a complimentary network for producing optimal queens?

If you desire raising queens for your own needs, or even marketing a few to sell, do not subscribe to the idea you need to pay big money for a "breeder" queen, at least not at this point in your beekeeping endeavor.

Prices for breeder queens run in the neighborhood of several hundred dollars. A breeder queen, usually instrumentally inseminated, is a genetic bank loaded with the wealth of the finest qualities and traits from which you want to raise your own queens, or more generally, queens to resell to other beekeepers.

Generally, those who sell large volumes of queens to other beekeepers buy an expensive breeder queen then produce hundreds of open-mated queens from this very special and valuable stock, marketed and sold, to beekeepers looking for certain traits for their production hives.

Breeder queens, by themselves, are not commonly used in simple production hives, rather, they are the source for raising volumes of high quality queens, generally on a commercial level of queen production. Commercial queen-rearing is a lot of work. The professionals in the queen production business make it look as easy as making a phone call.

Once you achieve a higher level of success in the beekeeper realm, once you develop a market for your queens, breeder queens might be an option, but my hunch is, at this point, probably not a prudent choice. Until you master the process of queen breeding, and I seriously mean *"master"* in the highest regard, breeder queens are not yet on your radar. Not only are they not on my radar, they're also not in my budget.

More often than I'm comfortable hearing, second- and third-year queen raisers who have picked up the knack of raising a handful of queens for their own use, ask me if I think they're ready to buy a breeder queen. They hope to start bringing in the *real* money selling queens.

If you wanted to concentrate and focus solely on queen breeding, putting all your eggs in this one basket, I might shrug and say, "It's a lot of money, really an investment. But if you think you are ready, then go for it. Nothing ventured, nothing gained. Let me know how I can help you."

I want to be encouraging and supportive of these aspiring queen producers, after all, we all have to start somewhere and everybody was a beginner once. So I may gently add a mild caveat to my encouragement, a little axiom my father taught me, "Those who have yet to learn how to cook should not buy expensive meat." If you catch my drift.

But there is so much more to selling queens commercially than buying a breeder queen. I have nothing but respect and admiration for my brothers and sisters in the commercial queen producing business, but developing a market, mastering the shipping complexities, replacing queens that show up dead on arrival...it's just too much for me.

I'm a honey producer. That's my purpose for keeping bees. I raise my own queens, not from expensive breeder stock, but from locally-adapted stock that tolerates my style of management. I'm all about the local component and sustainable concepts of what works for me in my little corner of the apicultural world. From time to time, I do buy mail-order queens to diversify my genetics.

If I wanted to start out selling queens on a commercial scale, I think I would opt for locally-adapted stock, restricting my sales territory to what beekeepers can drive and pick up when they buy their queens. I would over-winter these queens in nucs to provide for the market of local beekeepers who follow the dominant model of early spring splits. The queen-less nucs could be combined with a queen-right nuc for honey production.

Life is full of trade-offs and I don't suffer the concessions forced upon the commercial queen producers who know how to make the economies of scale work for them, which may not necessarily work for me.

I speak at conferences teaching local queen-rearing and promoting the NICOT system as the method of my choice. I believe we are moving further away from the dominant model of beekeeping to more sustainable practices, not so much by choice, but rather under the threat of our extinction as viable beekeepers.

Always remember the environment in which queens are raised makes a difference. Expensive breeding stock is not necessary, though obviously a bonus. Good nutrition is vital to good queens and will compensate for average genetics.

Obviously, great genetics and an optimal environment, together, hold the potential for the best results. For me, the trump card for raising local queens is waiting until the best nutritional environment exists, and for me, this is May and June.

Remember, as well, as I repeat this truth to hammer home its significance: nutrition, by my definition, must include a host of healthy, well-fed young nurse bees producing and feeding an abundance of royal jelly.

Without a doubt, in my opinion, waiting until the weather moderates and the nectar and pollen are flowing in abundance before I start raising my queens is my best option.

My success in raising queens comes from the cell builder colonies filled with young bees. I cannot discount the key factor of introducing age appropriate larvae, the younger the better in that 12- to 24-hour stage.

And let's not forget how the bees do all the work and it is rather arrogant for me to claim and credit this work as "my" success. I'm more of an errand boy.

When I create a queen-less environment, with incoming nectar and pollen, these young nurse bees are well fed, ready, willing, and more than able to feed developing larvae and convert them into high quality queens. The system works when I work.

What Else Makes for Great Queens?

Queen breeders quote a theory suggesting queens raised after June 21 (the "change of days" also called the summer solstice when our days start getting shorter) lay more eggs going into the winter than earlier queens raised before this date.

If this is true, then a hive headed by a young queen, actively laying more eggs going into the fall, brings a greater population of younger bees into the winter. Younger bees survive the winter better than older bees.

I also subscribe to a strongly held opinion that believes a queen overwintered in the hive is more productive than a newly-mated, southern-raised, mail-order queen installed in a split in the spring. This assumption mirrors the conclusion of much of Brother Adam's work at Buckfast Abbey.

I confess comparing these two scenarios of overwintered queens to early spring mail-order queens is like comparing apples and oranges. There really is no comparison. But if given the choice, I'll split my hives in the summer with my own, locally-adapted queens after the honey flow, in anticipation for the following season, rather than making splits in the early spring with mail-order queens raised in the south.

Further, younger, summer-raised queens brood up earlier in the spring of the subsequent year and hives headed by younger queens are less prone to swarm due to a more vibrant "queen substance."

There is a developing inclination toward annual requeening, and a growing trend for individuals to raise their own queens from their own locally-adapted stock. Local bee clubs and associations are looking to experienced beekeepers to raise queens for members with less experience. I've noticed a greater push to raising queens from "survivor" stock that may, or may not include a reduced-treatment regime, even a treatment-free philosophy.

The Real Challenge to Raising Your Own Queens

When you, as a beekeeper, take proactive responsibility for choosing the genetics of your queens, the quality of your apiaries improves, your productivity increases, and the winter losses decrease, when all other factors remain constant. I continue to contemplate what obstacles prevent more beekeepers from raising their own queens and taking control of these variables. The NICOT system distills the list of valid excuses to virtually nothing.

The hardest part of raising queens is counting the days and keeping the process on schedule. I created a simple spreadsheet on the computer to follow the days of preparation, the time the queen resides in the cell grid, and when I might expect capped queen cells. I cover this process in subsequent chapters.

Or use a simple calendar if you wish. Along with my computerized schedule (a print out goes with me to the bee yard), I track the same days from my spreadsheet on a desk-sized calendar hanging on the wall of my office.

The desk calendar gives me a different visual ans reminds me where things are at in the process, especially where I need to be in the progression of the developing queen cells. I cannot emphasize, enough, though the need to stay on schedule. If you want to raise queens, I encourage you to use whatever method works for you, and to try your absolute best to keep on schedule.

Once the queen-rearing train has left the station, you're committed to the schedule for the rest of the journey. The schedule is very unforgiving and if you mess up, you end up with larvae that are too mature or queens hatching and killing the other queens in the capped cells which have yet to emerge.

With that said, I find when I start the process of raising queens, it invariably rains for a week. The rain messes with the schedule and my access to the hives. I can almost guarantee it will rain torrents and I'll experience impassably muddy fields.

You need rain? Start raising queens.

But weather aside, if you can count days, you can raise queens using the NICOT system. If you can't count, plan on writing a check to a southern queen breeder and order your queens through the mail. Or encourage the members of your local association to raise you a few queens.

I believe your best bet is found in raising locally-adapted queens that fit your style of management.

It also pays to look at your personal calendar and adjust your queen rearing activities to avoid conflicts with family commitments and/or business obligations. It seems I'm in a time in my life when my children, including my nieces and nephews, are graduating, getting married and my wife wants to take in a few St. Louis Cardinal baseball games…and take me along!

Again, the hardest part is sticking to the schedule and dealing with the unpredictable weather and the intrusion of personal commitments. But actively planning ahead diminishes the impact of these unavoidable incidents, even the ones taking you by surprise. I still believe I can plan for the unplanned interruptions, but most things are easy enough to work around if you plan ahead and see them coming.

I'm always reminded it wasn't raining when Noah built the ark. Plan ahead.

Any Reasons Why You Shouldn't Raise Queens?

Queen rearing is not for everyone, but I have confidence that anyone can do it. When I ask beekeepers if they raise queens, especially from their own locally-adapted stock, the biggest excuse I hear is they don't know how to graft...as if grafting was the only method.

Don't worry. I don't know how to graft, either. With the NICOT kit, I don't have to know how to graft and I don't worry or lose sleep that I'll never bother to learn. You know what they say about teaching old dogs and they don't graft.

The industry standard and conventional expectation is the Doolittle method as the exclusive way to raise queens. Grafting is challenging to learn, but not impossible. I think people use their lack of grafting knowledge and/or skill as an excuse, but the NICOT system eliminates this problem.

Using a little common sense, I don't recommend first-year beekeepers raise queens until they acquire more experience and have sufficient hives to make mating nucs. While they can produce queen cells, the market for queen cells comes with an expiration date. Beginners could do it, but it would be a challenge.

Second, I hear people complain they don't have the time. It is true that queen rearing does take time, but not necessarily a quantity of time. There is a rigidity of the timing and a discipline required to stick to a schedule. If you are a procrastinator, queen-rearing probably isn't for you.

I've listened to people tell me they don't have enough hives to raise queens. I estimate, for every hive you wanted to split into mating nucs, you could raise four queens. So if you kept twelve colonies in your back yard, your maximum potential is likely limited to raising 48 queens. Obviously, this number is the high-end maximum and it's not likely you're in a position to do this.

If you only kept four hives, then your reasonable, upward limit is probably 16 queens...but there are many other variables, such as where you are going to place all these mating nucs? Jumping from four hives to sixteen hives is an aggressive move. Have you ordered enough frames and foundation to make this expansion a workable option?

People tell me they don't want to raise queens fearing they'll sacrifice their honey crop. This is true, but I have hives dedicated for honey production, and other hives dedicated for queen-rearing. I don't expect honey production from queen-rearing colonies.

Additionally, this is not a problem for me with my system of making nucs after the honey harvest in preparation for the subsequent season. I've heard people tell me it's just plain easier to pick up the phone, write a check, and order a queen through the mail.

This is true, but I've just experienced too many issues and variables with the quality and availability of my mail-order queens. Listening to the complaints at local bee meetings, I am under the impression beekeepers purchase mail-order queens just to insure they will always have something to complain about.

Most of all, I remain flabbergasted at the huge percentage of beekeepers who don't raise their own queens. I think the benefits far outweigh the challenges, the results far offset any excuse anyone can muster. The NICOT kit levels the playing field opening the door for the first-time queen producer to raise their own queens.

Chapter Seven:

Getting Down to Business:
Part I – The Simplified Explanation

The NICOT queen-rearing method utilizes two distinct hives. Beekeepers constantly ask me how many hives one needs to raise your own queens. What they are really asking is how *few* hives they need. Is there some magic number of hives required to raise queens?

The minimum is one, provided you know what you are doing. The single hive process utilizes a device called a Cloake board. If you want more information, running an Internet search provides the details.

I prefer two hives for the ease and efficiency of transferring larvae and convincing the bees of their need to build me queen cells.

Two hives accomplishes the first part of queen-rearing, producing queen cells. But the second part, inserting queen cells into mating nucs, requires more hives. If you raise several queens, you need additional hives to split up into mating nucs. The number of hives you need depends on how many queens you want to raise.

If you want to sell unhatched queen cells, then two is the minimum number of hives I would recommend. However, if you raise queens for yourself, my general rule of thumb is four queens raised for each healthy colony in your yard. Turning this statement around, each colony is split into four mating nucs, each to receive a ripe queen cell.

But you also need to take into account that producing four, capped, queen cells does not necessarily guarantee you'll have four mated queens at the end of the process. Just keep that in mind.

The next three sections will repeat the description of the NICOT process. First, I present a very simplified overview of how the kit works. Second, I go through the process, again, presenting a rough schedule that gives a little more detail and a loose idea on the timing. Third, with the foundational introduction of what I provided, I go into the "deep dive," repeating the process, again, only this time as a very detailed timetable arranges the fine points of how this system produces queens.

While you may accuse me of repeating myself, the simple overview evolves into the rough version, the rough version plows the path for the detailed method.

It's the same information presented three times, each time with more detail and depth.

This type of model was demonstrated to me when I took a biology class in college. The professor wanted to explain what happened on the cellular and molecular level on how food is converted to energy. She started out with the basics: you eat food, the body breaks it down, the gut absorbs what's needed and the bowels excrete and expel what's left.

Then she added, "And please wash your hands after doing so."

She moved to the deeper concepts of the same digestive process, showing how different organs worked together in the digestion system. She explained how the body responds to the presence of fats and sugars. We ended up with the Kreb's cycle and the eight steps of the aerobic process. That gave us the foundation to move into the understanding of ATP and ADP.

What I valued from her repetition was the developing context that provided layers of understanding beginning with the simple and working toward the complex.

This is my approach to explaining the NICOT queen-rearing kit. To merely explain the deeper details, and why you have to do what you have to do, can be confusing. So I'm going to start with a basic explanation, then repeat the explanation, moving into deeper details a second and third time.

My NICOT Kit Arrived: What's All This Stuff?

As my good buddy, Don Bennett likes to admonish, "There's a lot of moving parts to this thing." Well, there are a lot of parts. Thankfully, most of them don't move but they will roll off the workbench.

When you receive you NICOT kit, you'll find several components. Here's a quick listing of the parts, so as I mention them later, I want to give you an idea of what I'm talking about.

The cell grid: This is the heart of the NICOT system. The front looks like drawn comb. The back is the bottom end of the cells that make up the "comb."

On either side of the cell grid is a sheet of plastic foundation cut to fit the void on each side.

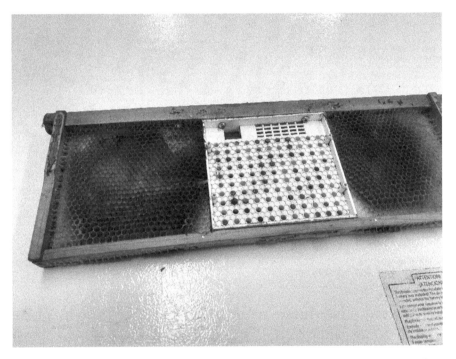

My NICOT kit: The cell grid fixed into a medium frame. The bees drew out the plastic foundation on both sides of the cell grid.

This is the front cover of the cell grid. It looks like a queen excluder that allows workers to enter, but keeps the queen contained. The little button on the top is the entrance hole for the queen to enter. The white cap is the door or gate.

It will also have a front that looks like a clear queen excluder, and a back that is a clear piece of plastic. The front will constrain the queen. The back keeps the cell cups from falling out.

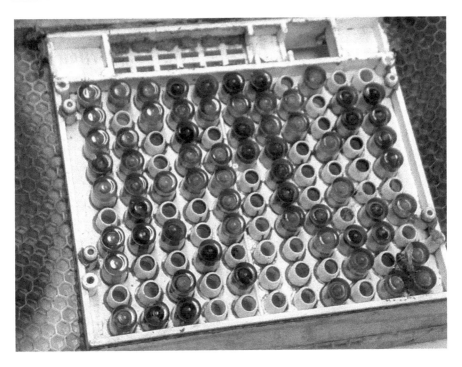

The back of the cell grid with some brown cell cups in place and some removed that had newly hatched larvae present.

The cell grid is also called the egg laying box or the comb box. There are 110 cells which means the maximum number of eggs the queen could lay is 110. However, not all 110 cell cups will produce queens.

I affixed my cell grid with flat-head sheet metal screws to a medium frame with a grooved (not wedge) top bar and a groove (not divided) bottom bar. The screws were ½″ long and I drilled holes in my cell grid to accommodate the screws.

The top edge of the cell grid affixed to the grooved top bar of the medium frame.

Brown Cell Cups: The cell cups fit on the back side of the cell grid. The queen will lay eggs into the cell, and they will adhere to the brown cell cup. The cell cup is transferred to another hive we call the cell builder once the egg has hatched into larva.

Brown cells cups that will be set on the back side of the cell grid, removed once the eggs hatch into the larval stage and transferred to the cell builder colony.

I will tell you on many occasions, you cannot transfer the brown cell cup to the cell builder if it still contains an unhatched egg. I know an "unhatched" egg is just an egg, but some people won't pay attention to me when I tell them transferring eggs is an exercise in futility. You can only transfer newly hatched larvae. Place the brown cell cups on the back side of the cell grid. Attach the back side which will be the solid cover.

Cell Cup Holder: This is a yellow-ish colored part that holds the cell cup. It should be obvious the smaller of the ends is where you slide in the cell cup once the larvae hatch.

On the right is the brown cell cup, and on the left is the cell cup holder in which the brown cell cup sits with a friction fit.

Cell Cup Fixture: Also known as a cell bar mount, these are dark brown in color with four tiny holes drilled into the four corners. These fixtures will fit onto the bottom side of your grooved top bar. I use standard, 18-guage, ¾" nails that come in small boxes from any hardware store or big box retailer like Lowe's or Walmart.

From left to right, 1) the cell cup fixture nailed to the grooved top bar of a medium frame, 2) the cell cup holder set on a cell cup fixture, and 3) the brown cell cup set into the cell cup holder. This frame is turned over and set into the space between two other frames of brood and bees in the queenless cell builder colony.

I nailed ten cell cup fixtures to my grooved top bars. Ten seemed to fit with enough space between them to get the cell cup holders on and off. To keep these frames properly spaced, I included a side bar. The bottom bar was not needed. You may see other frames with two or move levels to hold more cell cups. I just stuck with one level, just to keep things simple.

When the brown cell cups with newly hatched larvae are stuck into a cell cup holder, and the cell cup holder is attached to the cell cup fixture, the frame is ready to be placed into a queenless colony chock-full of young nurse bees and frames of pollen and nectar. Along the way, you may need one more part, the roller cages.

Roller Cages: The roller cages look like the old-fashioned hair rollers my mother used to put into her hair to create curls. Some catalogs call these hatching cages. These cages slide over a queen cell once it is fully developed and capped. The opening on the top will fit onto the upper part of the cell cup holder. With the end cap secured, these hatching cages retain a newly emerged queen.

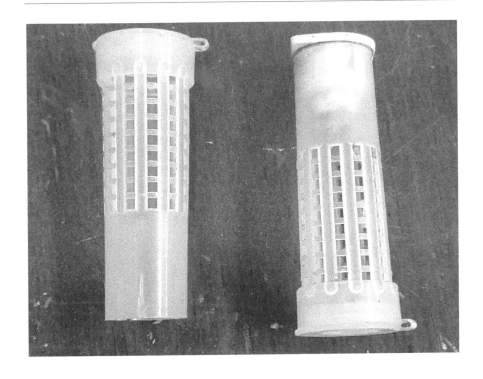

Roller cages, the one on the right shown with the cell cup
holder holding the roller cage in place.

Technically, in the vocabulary of entomologists, queens do not "hatch" like an egg. They "emerge" like an adult. When another beekeeper mistakenly uses the word, hatch, to describe their queens, I know what they mean, but the experts in this field are always kind enough to correct me when I'm asking them questions and mistakenly use the incorrect terminology.

The roller cage on a frame.

Retaining the queen provides you with two benefits. First, if you have not yet moved this queen cell to a mating nuc, you have a convenient way to do this instead of searching all over the cell builder for the newly emerged, virgin queen.

Second, the first virgin to emerge may go on a rampage destroying her "competition" in the adjacent queen cells. In this case, you have ten queen cells, and in short order, you have one queen.

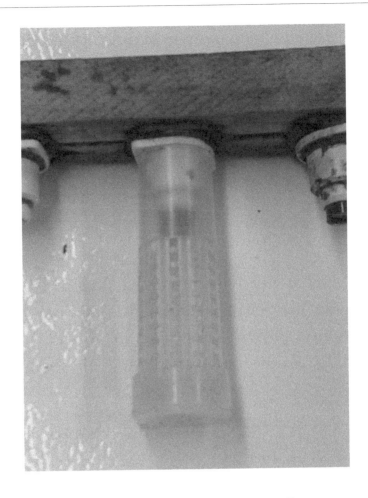

The roller cage set over a brown cell cup.

Sometimes the young nurse bees in a cell builder will recognize the overabundance of developing queens and they'll tear down what they consider to be excess queen cells. All my work is greatly diminished.

As I try and keep to my schedule, it has happened that a queen emerged a day, or even two days, ahead of my expected date. The newly emerged queen takes out the other queens.

Or a rain storm prevented me from getting into a bee yard and making mating nucs or transferring capped queen cells. The queens hatch and fight it out before I can get to them.

Or maybe my wife insisted I attend a baseball game with her because she finally got a day off and one of my grown kids was in town. There's something about that old mantra, "If mama ain't happy…"

Maybe it's "Happy spouse, happy house," because when I'm in a pissy mood, nobody else is having a happy birthday! Whatever the case may be, I often refer to these roller cages as "procrastination" cages. They protect my hard work from my idiotic procrastination.

But when a cell builder decides to take out six or seven capped queen cells. What's up with that? Was something wrong with those cells they tore down? Sometimes I wonder if they can recognize an inferior queen in the capped cell, or maybe they detect developing queens with issues that will later impact the colony. Maybe they are choosing a different larva somewhere else, instead of the ones in my cell cups, and they are telling me they already have a queen in the works so they don't need the larvae I gave them.

I don't know. I often use my default response that we need to trust the bees as they often know more than us. Still, I use the roller cages to protect capped queen cells.

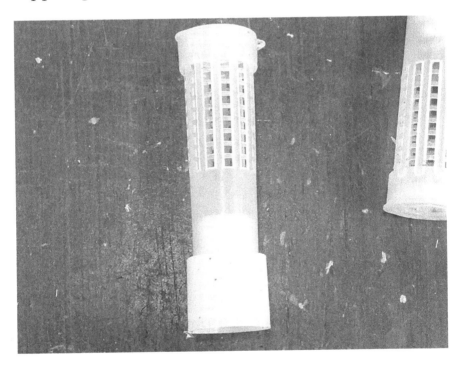

The roller cage with a candy plug.

Roller cages also come with another end that can be filled with a candy plug for introducing the queen. The idea is the bees eat out the candy plug, and by the time they do, they are familiar with the queen's pheromones.

As for my operation, I have found great success in releasing a newly hatched virgin directly into a queenless mating nuc without a candy plug. Her pheromones are not yet developed and she can start maturing in preparation for her mating flight. When I tried the roller cages to introduce a virgin queen, they often ignored her and she starved. I have my mating nucs ready to go prior to my queen emerging. When I open the cell builder and find a newly hatched queen, she goes directly into a mating nuc.

I have used these roller cages to sell queens and used the candy plug on the end. I find when I go into a nuc to find a queen to sell, it is far easier, with less threat of injuring the queen, to get her into this roller cage than trying to grab her and coax her into a conventional, three-hole shipping cage.

More on how these things all work together as I explain the system.

So What Do You Need? The Simplified Overview

First, I need two hives. I prepare the first hive to be queenless (without a queen) and broodless (no open brood, larvae or eggs). **This is my cell builder colony**. This hive is full of young bees to feed royal jelly to newly hatched larvae, converting them into queens, and in the process, builds queen cells, hence the name, "cell builder."

Prior to introducing the newly hatched larvae to this cell builder colony, I manipulate the hive so it develops into a broodless and queenless environment. These two conditions are required to inspire the young nurse bees to make queen cells.

There are a couple of ways to do this and I'll explain what works for me in more detail in the next few pages. Basically, I modify the organization of the frames and create an environment that lacks a queen, and where no open larvae can be made into queens.

This is the definition of broodless and queenless.

Then, when I introduce newly hatched larvae, there are no other options than to feed the young larvae I have given them. The young nurse bees eagerly feed copious amounts of royal jelly and convert the larvae into queen cells. It's pretty simple, but you have to know *what* you are doing and *why* you are doing it. It also helps to know *when* to do these steps.

The second hive I need is a normally functioning, **queen-right colony**. This colony produces the larvae I transfer to the cell builder colony. This is the productive, gentle colony I really admire, likely from last season, and I want more queens just like the one heading up this colony. We all have differing criteria of what constitutes a nice queen. The idea is to pick a queen which works for you and helps meet your goals as a beekeeper.

Taking the NICOT queen-rearing kit, I place several cell cups on the back side of the egg laying box (also called the "cell grid"). I catch the queen from my queen-right colony, and then release her into the cell grid where she is confined. I insert this frame holding the cell grid back into my queen-right colony.

This means I need to remove a frame to make room, but a word to the wise: Because the cell grid is slightly wider than a frame, I remove two frames to give the bees full access to the front of the cell grid.

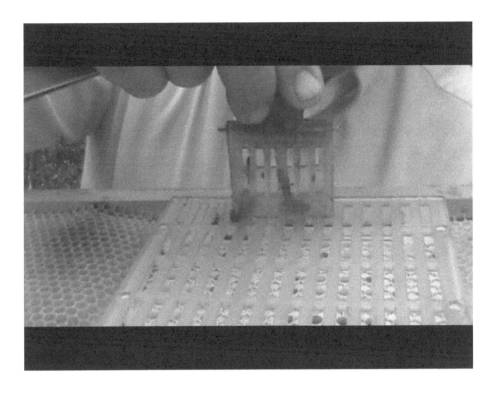

Photo: Releasing the queen from my queen catcher into the hole in the front cover of the egg laying box (the cell grid). Once inside, I replace the plug and confine her to the cell grid.

I patiently wait a few days allowing the queen to lay eggs into the cell cups. Eggs take three-and-a-half days to hatch. So there is no point in opening this colony until four days later.

Once these eggs hatch into larvae, I transfer the cell cups from the cell grid in this queen-right colony to a special frame. I previously nailed, to this frame, specialized cell cup fixtures to receive the cell cups.

The cell cups are physically removed from the cell grid and transferred (with the larvae intact) to the cell cup fixtures with the use of the cell cup holders. I nailed ten fixtures on each top bar frame.

Photo: This is the back side of the cell grid with the rear cover removed. In the cell cup on the left, the little dot of royal jelly highlights the presence of a hatch larva. On the right, an egg. Even with modestly poor vision, finding the age appropriate larvae is easy. Transferring eggs to the cell builder is futile.

I place two or three, maybe four, top bar frames holding ten cell cups into the queenless cell builder colony and let the bees do the heavy lifting.

Photo: The top bar frames, painted purple, the color of "royalty," with cell cups attached. These frames look white in this black and white picture. Note the alternating pattern of top bars with cell cups with frames of pollen and nectar. Not all forty cell cups will be converted into queen cells.

Since the cell builder colony contains no brood and no queen, the bees joyfully, though dutifully, feed royal jelly and raise queen cells from the larvae on the frames I transfer to it.

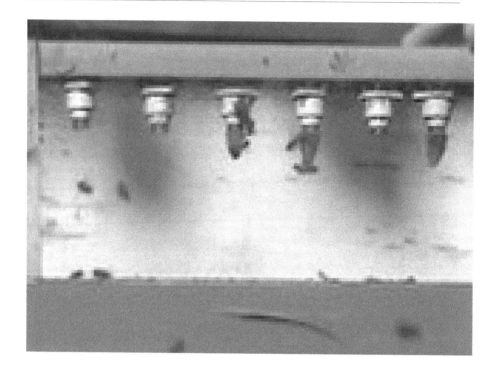

Photo: The picture is rather grainy, but you can see a portion of the top bar frame showing six of the ten yellow cell cup holders. From the left side, there are two vacant cell cups which the bees did not convert into queen cells. In the middle, there are two capped queen cells, followed by a vacant cell (sometimes we call them "blanks"), and on the far right another capped queen cell.

In a week or so, I normally find capped queen cells. The key to the queenless cell builder colony is to have plenty of young nurse bees, ample nectar, and pollen. Nutrition makes good queens and you need well-fed nurse bees which feed the developing larvae.

Once the cell builder seals and caps the queen cells, I make up my mating nucs and transfer individual queen cells to each respective mating nuc before the cells hatch.

If I should procrastinate and all the queen cells are together in the cell builder colony, it's very probable the first queen to emerge will go down the line of sealed queen cells and kill off all her competition. This effectively ends all my prior work and I'm back to square one.

What did I say about procrastination in queen-rearing?

Once the mating nucs are made up and given a queen cell, I give the queens 14 days to emerge, mature, mate and settle down before I reopen the mating nuc to see if she's laying eggs. If I can't find any eggs, I give the queen another week for a second inspection. Once she starts laying eggs, I'll mark that queen with the color appropriate to the year.

The process is very simple. If you can count the days on the calendar, and if you can adhere to the schedule, you can raise queens. Actually, the bees raise the queens for you. Don't take too much credit for your results.

Chapter Eight:

Part II -- The Rough Schedule

Here is another way of looking at the same process with more depth and detail. To keep the schedule simple, and to give you a generalized overview of what we're doing with the NICOT system, I present a very rough, cursory schedule with a few more specifics than the simplified overview.

If you can understand the basics of the simple schedule, and what we do to manipulate the colonies to prepare for the process, the rough schedule starts tweaking the details.

This can be confusing. After the rough schedule, I'll follow with the detailed plan. The success of the NICOT system is found in the details.

The game plan in this book is to repeat the description of the process that I outlined in the simplified process. Let's look a little closer how this NICOT system works by filling in some of the cracks.

My queen-rearing schedule can start on any day of the week, but the counting of the days in the queen-rearing process starts five days before the queen goes in the cell grid to lay eggs. There are a few things that need to be in place prior to expecting the queen to lay eggs in the cell grid.

The day when the queen is placed into the cell grid and confined to lay eggs, is the day when things really get rolling, so I like to think of this as Day 0. The days that lead up to this day are preparation days.

By setting this particular day at Day 0 also then coordinates the process with the queen's developmental stages.

I'm going to start with two colonies, 1) a queenright colony as the source of my age-appropriate larvae, and 2) a cell builder colony that will take those larvae and convert them into queen cells.

Here is how I manipulate the **queenright colony**.

Day -5 Nothing to do.

Day -2 I remove two frames from the sides of the brood box and create a vacancy in the middle of the brood nest for the cell grid. The cell grid is placed into this vacancy without the front attached, and without placing the queen in it. This timing is to allow the workers to polish the cell cups and to allow the cell grid to "warm up."

Day 0 I place the front cover on the cell grid and slip the queen into the cell grid to lay eggs in the brown cell cups.

Day 4 I look for newly-hatched larvae. If they are present, I transfer the cell cups with the newly-hatched larvae to the cell builder colony. The queen can be released from the cell grid.

If I have a sufficient number brown cell cups with newly-hatched larvae, I can take out the cell grid and return the two frames I removed on Day -2.

Here is how I manipulate the **cell builder colony,** which also takes place at the same time.

Day -5 I isolate the queen to create part of the brood nest that will become broodless over the next nine days.

Day 4 The brood box with the queen is removed. I transfer cell cups with newly-hatched larvae from the queenright colony into the cell builder colony.

Day 10 I can expect to find capped queen cells.

Day 12 I make up my mating nucs and distribute the queen cells.

Day 16 Queen cells hatch. The virgins mate and commence laying eggs, shortly.

Day 28 I confirm the presence of a mated queen in the mating nuc.

If I were to lay out the two colonies on a spreadsheet, side-by-side, it would look like this:

	A	B	C	D	E	F	G	H
1	Date	Day	Cell Builder Colony			Queenright Colony		
2								
3		-5	Isolate Queen					
4		-4						
5		-3						
6		-2				Insert Cell Grid into brood area		
7		-1						
8		0				Insert Queen into Cell Grid		
9		1						
10		2						
11		3						
12		4	Remove Queen			Transfer Newly Hatched Larvae		
13		5				Release Queen From Cell Grid		
14		6						
15		7						
16		8						
17		9						
18		10	Expect Capped Queen Cells					
19		11						
20		12	Make Up Mating Nucs					
21		13	Transfer Capped Queen Cells					
22		14						
23		15						
24		16	Expect Queens to Hatch					

One of the tricks for understanding the NICOT system is remembering which colony has the queen (the queenright colony) and which colony becomes queenless (the cell builder colony).

So How Are These Two Colonies Set Up?

When I start preparing for this process, the beginning is Day (-5), or a "negative" five. I start five days before I put the queen in the cell grid, Day 0. But there are a few things that need to happen first.

Five days before we want the queen to lay eggs in our cell grid (that box with the cell cups inserted on the back side), we prepare another colony to become a queenless, broodless colony to convert our larvae into queens and build queen cells. This is my cell builder colony.

In the cell builder colony, with no queen and no open brood, we force the colony to accept our newly hatched larvae (transferred from the cell grid in the queenright colony) and, in return, the bees gladly feed ample amounts of royal jelly to these larvae in order to produce queen cells.

The queenless situation obligates the bees in the cell builder colony to make a queen, for without a queen, the colony is doomed. Those young nurse bees know their future rides on their ability to convert age appropriate larvae into queen cells.

As the cell builder colony is set up, I manipulate the frames so there are no available larvae to make into a queen. Fortunately, when I want to raise queen cells, all I need to do is supply the cell builder colony with newly hatched larvae.

I often refer to larvae that have recently hatched, like in the last 24- to 36-hours, as "age-appropriate." These larvae come from the queenright colony. All I have to do is transfer the age-appropriate larvae from the queenright colony into the cell builder.

Because there are no other age-appropriate larvae in this cell builder colony, the bees will build queen cells only on the frame I give them which is right where I want these queen cells built, and nowhere else.

Given several larvae to choose from, it is not uncommon for the cell builder to make multiple queen cells...and this is, obviously, highly desirable.

So five days prior to placing the queen from the queenright colony in the cell grid, it's Day -5 and I begin the process of preparing the cell builder to become queenless and broodless. In all, this process to reach a broodless and queenless state will take a total of nine days. Keep that little detail in mind.

Nine days later, on Day 4, larvae from the cell grid in the queenright are transferred to this queenless, broodless, cell builder colony.

If I were to install a queen excluder between two, stacked, brood boxes, the eggs and larvae in the brood box without a queen will soon mature to the pupae stage and become inaccessible for making into a queen cell. They can still smell and sense the queen in the other brood box and workers can move freely through the queen excluder.

When I take away the brood box with the queen, the bees in the other box sense her absence and start looking for newly-hatched larvae to make into queen cells. But there are none available.

When I transfer age-appropriate larvae from my queenright colony, the cell builder colony makes queen cells exactly where I want them because they are on the frame with the cell cups.

After initially setting up my cell builder colony on Day -5, I switch my attention from this cell builder to the queen-right colony to prepare this colony to receive the cell grid where the queen will lay eggs.

I let three days pass since I initialized the cell builder colony. There is nothing more to do in that colony, so my focus shifts to the other colony, my queen-right colony. It's two days before our queen enters the cell grid. This is Day -2.

On this day, before the cell grid goes into the queen-right colony I fill up the entire back side of the cell grid with cell cups. Even if you don't need 110 queens, go ahead and put all the cell cups on the back side of the cell grid. I put the back cover on the cell grid which keeps all the cell cups in place.

I do not put the queen in the cell grid, not just yet. I do not put the front cover (slotted) on the cell grid, at least, not yet. Without the cover, I give workers full, unencumbered access to polish the brown cell cups and make them more desirable for the queen.

I place the cell grid (with cups, no front cover) into my queen-right colony between two frames of open brood. The nurse bees will sense the cell grid and begin to prepare it and allow it to "warm up." To make room for the cell grid, I need to take out two frames from the far edges of this brood box.

I let two days pass, which brings me to Day 0.

On Day 0, I return to the queen-right colony and catch my queen. I put the front cover on the cell grid, and release the queen into the cell grid to lay eggs.

Technically, it's now five days since I started the process, but I want to keep the "count of the days" on the same timeline as the developing larvae, thus the queen goes into the cell grid on Day 0. Since I know the queen cells will emerge on Day 16, any manner of counting the days of the process will work, as long as you keep in mind when the queen cells get capped and when you have to have the mating nucs ready.

An egg takes three and a half days to hatch. Thus, nothing happens over the course of the next four days. There is nothing to do in the queen-right colony. The cell builder colony is doing its thing allowing the brood to mature, so there is nothing to do here, either, except keep track of the days on the schedule.

On Day 4, I come back to the queen-right colony and check to see if the queen laid any eggs and, more importantly, to see if those eggs have hatched into young larvae. Sometimes I only find eggs. If the queen laid eggs on Day 0, then on Day 4, I should find newly hatched larvae.

But the queen may not have laid eggs on her first day in the cell grid. She may not have laid eggs on the second day. This means when I show up and inspect the cell grid and find unhatched eggs, I have not reached Day 4.

Day 4 is not necessarily a day on the calendar. Day 4 is a developmental stage in the life of the developing larvae. This required a shift of perspective on my part. There is a fourth day on the calendar, but Day 4 with newly hatched larvae is what moves us forward.

Because the process of raising queens requires a strict schedule, it is the presence of young larvae defines Day 4. If I only find eggs, then it is still Day 3. If I come back the following day and only find eggs, it is still Day 3.

The schedule is strict, but also requires flexibility to adjust as we wait for the newly hatched larvae to appear. As long as you find eggs when you look at the back of the cell grid, the count is put on hold. You can be stuck on Day 3 for a couple of physical, calendar days. The green light to move forward is the day you find newly hatched larvae.

In the life of those developing queens, Day 4 is when the egg hatches and the larva begins its journey. Day 4 is when you transfer the cell cup from the cell grid to the cell builder.

Here's where this method confuses other beekeepers. Until I discover the presence of larvae, the schedule is put on hold. It can be Day 3 for several days. Only when I find newly hatched larvae, the schedule moves to Day 4

Okay, so why is it such a big deal to wait for the larvae to show up? Why can't we just plow on through as if it were Day 4?

Because the queen may balk at laying eggs when first released into the confinement of the cell grid, it is very possible she'll wait for a day or two before laying eggs. If she waits a couple of days, then Day 4 is delayed a couple of days.

Until I find newly hatched larvae, the day count is temporarily suspended until I do find larvae. If I fail to find larvae, I make plans to return the next day to check again see if I have larvae.

If not this day, I return the next day, and if not on this next day, then I return on the next day after that day until I find larvae. Eventually, you'll find hatching eggs and brand new larvae.

Here is a key point to the success of the NICOT system. At the risk of being repetitive, I cannot stress this point enough: If there are no larvae, the count of the days is suspended. The earliest presence of larvae resets the schedule at Day 4.

Here is where my spread sheet or calendar needs some flexibility to allow for the "limbo" days.

On Day 4, when it finally arrives, I transfer the cell cups with newly hatched larvae from the cell grid to the top bar frames with the cell cup fixtures, and these top bar frames go into my cell builder colony. I can only transfer newly hatched larvae, and once I do, the schedule will tell me when they are ready to come out of the cell builder.

If there is some good news, once I find newly hatched larvae, the schedule switches from marking time with "limbo" days to the lock-step, unforgiving schedule that proceeds like a run-away freight train on a downhill slope. When I say there is no room for procrastination, there is no room.

On Day 10, I should have capped queen cells. I count the number of sealed cells telling me how many mating nucs to prepare. Each capped queen cell needs a mating nuc. The number of capped queen cells varies from one cell builder to the next, so a count is always necessary prior to assembling my mating nucs. The cell builder colony will not convert every larvae into a queen cell. Expect to find a few vacant cell cups or "blanks."

Photo: Here is one of the greatest joys coming out of the cell builder colony: ten capped queen cells. As I pull this out on Day 10, this informs me I need to get ten mating nucs ready. This frame is returned to the cell builder colony until the mating nucs are made up. These cells hatch on Day 16.

On Day 11, it's time to make up the mating nucs, and I need to inspect the frames that go into the mating nuc to insure I don't accidentally include the queen. I allow 24- to 48-hours of queenlessness to prepare the mating nuc to receive the capped queen cell. I gather frames from my existing hives and make my nucs. Pulling a couple of frames from a hive will not hurt a normal colony.

On Day 13, I like to plant my queen cells in the mating nucs, tucking them in between two frames of brood.

By Day 16, I expect emerging queens. Sometimes in the heat of summer, they come out on Day 15 so I like to be a little ahead of schedule. When I pick my newly hatched larvae, the oldest ones hatch first, so I want to include a little margin to buffer my stupidity. Again, keep in mind not every queen cell hatches.

By Day 28, maybe even a little earlier, I expect to see eggs if the queen successfully returned from her mating flight. I remind myself not to get too optimistic as I open the mating nucs. Some of the virgin queens don't always make it back from their mating flights! My advice to potential queen raisers is this: Do not count your chicks, or in this case, queens, until they hatch, mate and start to lay eggs in your mating nuc! Raising queens encounters several layers of attrition.

If I open the mating nuc and have no eggs, but I still see a queen running around, I come back in seven days to give the mating nuc a second inspection. If there are no eggs at the second inspection, something didn't go right.

My options are now to either combine this failed nuc with a successfully mated queen in another mating nuc, or to insert another queen cell from another round of queen rearing, provided I have another batch coming along.

The Detailed Plan

So that's the rough schedule. If the third time's the charm, here's a look at the same schedule, again, only this time employing more of the nitty-gritty details and the blow-by-blow, play-by-play steps making the NICOT system such a joy to use. These are also the details that make the NICOT system work, and when it works, it's a joy!

Given the details necessary to raise queens, given a couple of steps required to make the NICOT system work, you may not experience the joy if you attempt some short-cuts. But trust me. The effort is worth it. Pay attention to the details.

Chapter Nine:

Hacking the NICOT System

Okay, so after laying out the rough schedule, I am personally exhausted. The details required of the NICOT queen-rearing system are almost enough to make me learn how to graft larvae.

Almost.

There is way to short-cut the system and override the details, but only in part. The short-cut, known in today's vocabulary as "a hack," may not produce the same results as paying attention to the details. Which begs the question of whether or not the hack is worth pursuing? Is the cost of paying attention to the details worth the benefit, or can we find a way to experience a gain without so much pain?

Life is complicated and beekeepers are busy, as am I. So before I launch into my third explanation and the detailed plan, I offer a "cheat-code," something to help you get passed some of the excruciating details.

I confess, I discovered this hack by accident. As time was slipping away one summer, I needed queens. Every day I didn't start the NICOT process was another day lost. Out of desperation, I cheated. While I'm not proud of cheating, I was rather impressed with the results. Here's what I did.

Rather than set up the cell builder colony on Day -5, I jumped right into the queenright colony and prepared the cell grid for the queen. This would have been my normal Day -2.

I opened up a really nice colony that was headed by a productive queen that I wanted to produce daughters. Removing two frames from outer sides that were essentially ignored, I created a two-frame space in the heart of the brood nest, where the young workers hang out.

Into this vacancy, I inserted my cell grid with the brown cell cups inserted on the back side. The back cover was in place to keep the brown cell cups from falling out. The front side was open to give full access to the workers.

I left the cell grid in place for two days to warm up. This step is hard to hack as placing a queen into a cold cell grid with unpolished cups really takes away her enthusiasm to lay eggs. It's hard enough to entreat her to accommodate my schedule with a warmed up cell grid, so this is not a step to try and hack.

After two days, essentially forty-eight hours, I returned and located my marked queen. Placing the front on the cell grid to confine the queen, I released the queen into the cell grid. I marked this day on my calendar.

I came back four days later. I found no newly-hatched larvae, so I closed up the colony. I came back the next day. I still found unhatched eggs. When I came back the next day, which was six days after releasing the queen, I found thirteen, newly-hatched larvae.

Because I checked every day, I am very confident these larvae were, at most, less than twenty-four hours old. This is an ideal state to transfer them to a cell builder colony.

For a cell builder colony, I approached a nice colony that was started as a nuc, earlier that spring. It had grown to a two brood boxes. I removed two frames and the queen to a nuc box, essentially making it queenless. This nuc box was moved to a different bee yard and fed with the hopes of making it through the coming winter.

I created two vacancies in the heart of the brood nest which were not side-by-side. I created this vacancy by removing the existing queen and two frames to the nuc box.

I took my brown cell cups with the newly-hatched larvae and slid them into the cell cup holders on two frames I use for my NICOT system. I placed them into this queenless colony. I made a notation in my notebook, that on this day, newly-hatched larvae were transferred, or in the language of experienced beekeepers, the larvae were "grafted." I could expect capped queen cells one week later. So I made that notation in my notebook.

At this juncture, it would not be uncommon to experience the roar of objections from beekeepers who are quick in their rush to express their opinions. They would say this colony is not broodless and I did not give them enough time of being queenless for them to turn my grafted larvae into queen cells. They might conclude the workers will take older larvae from the existing frames rather than accept my grafts.

Well, apparently this colony did not listen to the detractors. Because the colony was queenless, the young nurse bees shifted their priorities to converting the larvae normally destined as workers into queen cells. Because I gave them newly-hatched larvae placed them in a vertical orientation, the young nurse bees appeared to prefer the grafted larvae, as opposed to reconstructing the horizontal cells in the frames into queen cells. This colony also had a nice population of young nurse bees as well as ample nectar and pollen to feed the larvae.

I came back to the cell grid on each of the next two days and repeated the process of transferring newly-hatched larvae into a regular colony in which I had just removed the queen and two frames of bees to a nuc box. After the third transfer, I released the queen from the cell grid and returned the two frames previously removed to accommodate the cell grid.

I had three queenless colonies in which I grafted newly-hatched larvae, each one day ahead of the other. The workers accepted those grafts and made half of them into capped queen cells. I had no queen cells constructed on the existing frames. From there I made up some mating nucs and dispersed the capped queen cells.

This little experiment produced three batches of queen cells, all one day apart. I left two queen cells in each of these cell builder colonies to account for the queen and two frames of brood I used to make nucs.

I stumbled upon this hack at a time when I was overwhelmed with tasks and short on time. I was frazzled. I didn't have the mental capacity to count the days of the process and prepare a cell builder colony in the proper sense. I took my chances and trusted the bees. They came through for me. Maybe they felt sorry for me and decided to cooperate.

If this little experiment had failed, I still had my back-up plan to call a queen producer and order mated queens. What made this hack work is that I already had an understanding of what was required of a colony to take newly hatched larvae and convert them into queen cells. It was not a hack of wishful thinking that defied the common sense fundamentals of honey bee biology.

Always remember, the methods may vary but the principles never change.

Chapter Ten:

The Detailed Plan

So why explain the NICOT system a third time? When I've taught queen-rearing, especially in instances using this method, a front-to-back general overview helps acquaint the student with the all-purpose process. But an overview won't give you the level of success you're expecting. The overview lays down the basics of **what** happens.

The second time brings in most of the details that fill in the gaps, but many aspects are still missing. The NICOT system is uniquely different and hearing it a second time brings clarity to **how** it works.

The third time, while sounding redundant, sheds light on **why** it works. Failing to understand **what** I'm doing, **how** I'm doing it and **why** this method requires me to do certain things only brings frustration to those who think it should be easy.

The frustration experienced by other beekeepers, and myself when I attempted my first stab at raising some queens is, unfortunately, quite common. We simply failed and came up empty.

I like what my buddy, Bruce Snavely says about failing: It's just the tuition we pay to go to bee school. Failure is an opportunity to learn something a different way.

This, again, gets me back to the purpose of writing this book, namely, to help you find the level of success you hope for. The longer I keep bees, the more convinced I become regarding the importance of the queen and her youthful vitality to my success as a beekeeper.

In several of the conferences I've attended, speakers cite the results of several studies and surveys raising the reasons why colonies fail. The consistent cause at the top of every list is queen quality (i.e., poor queens, short-lived queens, premature supersedure, laying workers usurping the colony, shotgun patterns, low productivity, poor matings). And let's face it, when you have a bad queen, for whatever reason, additional problems with the hive start lining up, ready to fall like a row of dominoes.

This NICOT method of raising queens works, but it works in a very specific, certain, narrow way. When I pay attention, take care, and follow the particular steps, successfully raising my own queens brings incredible results, and results give me satisfaction.

Further, the benefits of my locally-adapted queens elevate the productivity and profitability of my honey production. Now I'm ecstatic, and I gratefully acknowledge how my jubilation resides in the quality of my queens, which is a level of quality I control. Sustainable beekeeping reduces the variables. But you can't get there unless you understand how the NICOT system works. There are no shortcuts.

The third time explaining the NICOT system is like building a salad. The first explanation was like the croutons and the bacon bits. They're nice, but hardly filling. The second explanation was the grated cheese and sliced deviled eggs, maybe a cucumber slice. Now were getting some flavor. The third explanation is the lettuce, spinach, greens and probably some artichoke hearts. Now we got the important stuff, the foundational base upon which allows the grated cheese, eggs, bacon bits, croutons, and everything else we forgot to sit.

Six Basic Steps to the Nicot System

There are six basic steps to raising queens using the Nicot Queen Rearing Kit.

- ✓ First, organize the hive which will be your cell builder colony,

- ✓ Second, prepare the cell grid for the queen to lay eggs. The cell grid goes in the queenright colony,

- ✓ Third, put the queen in the cell grid,

- ✓ Fourth, transfer the newly hatched larvae from the cell grid to the cell builder colony,

- ✓ Fifth, prepare the mating nucs and transfer the capped queen cells,

- ✓ Sixth, check for queen acceptance and mating success.

How to Stay on Schedule

I create a computerized spread sheet, and carry a plain calendar to keep me on track. When I'm juggling a couple of rounds of queens, I sometimes wake up in the middle of the night with the single-focused, disturbing trepidation: "What day is it?"

My wife mumbles, "Check the calendar and go back to sleep."

A good system of counting the days lets me sleep at night. The queen-rearing schedule is a stern taskmaster, inviolately unforgiving unless one learns to surrender to the demands of the process. There is no room for grace or mercy, and no reason for the schedule to absolve your procrastination. One of the components I tend to preach over and over is the need to stay on schedule.

No exceptions. No excuses.

There is no room for procrastination and some days the calendar forces me out to a bee yard in the driving rain to making things happen because I am on a schedule. On more than one occasion, I erected my 10' by 10' tent, the one I use at the farmer's market, over the hive to keep me (relatively) dry and (hopefully) placate the bees while I worked.

My wife thought I was crazy. I countered with, "Crazy is just another word for dedicated."

She didn't buy it and responded, "Dedicated is another word for committed, and you need to be committed to the insane asylum."

Create whatever system works for you. Count the days and stay on schedule. Let's see how this schedule shapes up and how it works.

Day -5:

Five days before I want the queen to start laying eggs, that is, five days before the queen goes into the cell grid, I begin preparing my cell builder colony. This is the colony which will eventually be broodless and queenless and convert my newly hatched larvae into queen cells.

I start this procedure on this day because it has to be done in advance, and because I need a minimum of nine total days to pass, allowing any and all existing eggs in the cell builder colony to hatch and mature into the pupal stage.

The cell builder colony must be "broodless" (no open, uncapped larvae) so the bees direct all their energy to the newly hatched larvae I transfer from the cell grid. The cell grid goes into that other hive, the queen-right colony, on Day -2.

In reality, Day -5 is really the first day of this process, but I want to coordinate the actual days with the larval development, and since the cell builder has to be prepared five days in advance, we thus start on day -5, or day, "negative five."

I head out into my bee yard or I look over my notes from the previous year and designate which hive I want to be my cell builder colony to raise new queens. This colony should be healthy and robust with a good laying queen and lots of brood, a strong population of bees and incoming nectar and pollen. It is my preference to choose four colonies to become my cell builder colonies.

With a little luck, I might make the process work with one hive, but four hives provides insurance for more opportunities for making queens. And, as these colonies need to be prepared in advance, if something goes wrong with one of the cell builder hives, I don't have to take the process back to square one.

I start preparing one of these hives as a queenless, broodless cell builder colony by choosing a healthy, strong hive made up of two brood boxes. It might have supers on top of the brood boxes which will help alleviate the swarming impulse, but for the sake of illustration, consider the following picture.

Photo: For my cell builder colonies, I start with a healthy hive with lots of bees, a good laying queen, and lots of brood. Conceivably, this could be a good honey producing colony, but I'm going to dedicate it to raising queen cells for me.

I manipulate and reorganize the frames in both boxes, and sort into the bottom brood box the frames of sealed brood, older brood, along with any frames of brood containing ample stores of nectar/honey and pollen.

Photo: Once the brood frames have been sorted, a queen excluder is inserted and the queen is placed in the upper brood box. Note the white line between the two boxes. That's the queen excluder.

At the same time, I sort frames of open brood and the empty frames into the top brood box.

In this process of sorting frames, I keep an eye out for the queen. If you mark your queens, they'll be easier to find. Once I find my queen, I constrain her temporarily in a queen catcher. The queen catcher I prefer is the spring-loaded, "clam shell" type of clear plastic that allows me to pick up the queen off the comb without injury. These are available from most beekeeping supply catalogs.

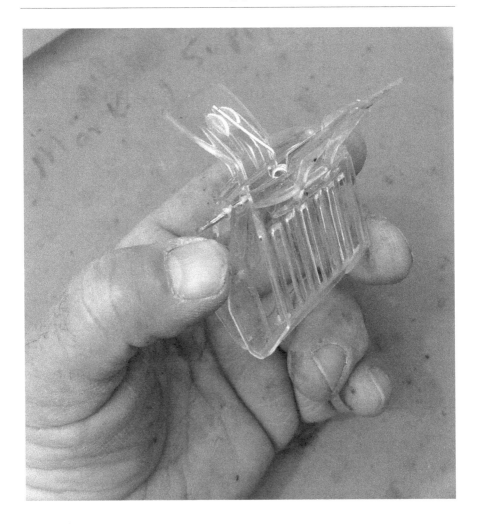

I reassemble the colony, and divide the bottom box (sealed brood) and the top box (open brood) with a queen excluder. I release the queen into the <u>upper</u> box.

I repeat this manipulation on three more hives for a total of four, cell builder colonies.

The significance of establishing a cell builder colony in this manner isolates certain frames in the lower box and confines the queen to the upper box. I effectively prevent the queen from laying any new eggs in this lower brood box, and at the same time, allow the existing larvae in this lower box to mature beyond the point where they can be turned into queen cells.

After nine days, all the eggs in this lower box hatch and all the larvae pupate into sealed brood. Over these nine days, I successfully create a "broodless" (meaning no "open" brood) box. My suggestion, again, is to convert four different hives to act as cell builder colonies.

> **_Side Note_**: You may be able to get by with one cell builder colony. But since these colonies need to be set up in advance, it is a good idea to set up four. If it turns out you don't need them, you can simply remove the queen excluder and return them to their normal function. If, for some reason, one of the cell builders does not work out, or in the event you messed up, you have not lost any ground. You do not need to

start from scratch and you've not lost any time. Have I suggested that time is money? (Yes!)

Day -2:

It's still two days before I catch the queen and release her into the cell grid. My attention shifts from the cell builder colony to my queen-right colony which raises my larvae destined to become queens.

I choose a colony from which I want to raise more queens, hopefully capturing the same favorable genetic attributes, and charming characteristics of the existing queen I so greatly admire. This is not an exact science, but chose a queen that works for you, in your area, under your management, as I've mentioned before.

Thankfully, each season I keep copious notes so I know which surviving hives fit my rationale from which to raise queens each season. One of my reasons for keeping notes every season is to identify potential colonies as possibilities for producing future queens.

I choose a prosperous, healthy colony that fits my ideals of honey production, gentleness, or whatever criteria I see working for me. Surviving my management ranks high on my selection scale. I confess, I prefer the darker queens and color is completely superfluous as a serious consideration. Obviously, your criteria will vary based on your purpose for keeping bees.

My main purpose is honey production, and I'll use performance as my criteria. Most people tell me they want to choose to raise queens from "gentle" hives. Always remember our genetic selection, given the randomness of open mating, is kind of iffy, and somewhat beyond our control.

On this day, Day -2, I insert the cell grid into my queen-right colony for the express purpose of inviting the bees to clean up, polish, and prepare the cell cups for the queen.

Without this step, the queen will not find the cell cups in the cell grid acceptable and you'll just waste more time, generating more frustration, falsely concluding these plastic contraptions don't work. They work, when you work, and follow the little details.

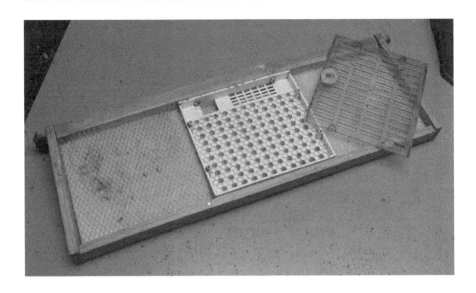

Photo: The cell grid, actually the egg laying box, is attached to a medium frame, and two panels of plastic foundation are cut to fit the two sides. Here we see the front cover removed.

I prepare the cell grid by attaching the unit to the top bar and the bottom bar of a medium frame, and to make the box sit square, I use a frame with a grooved top and grooved bottom bars (not wedge top or divided bottom bars).

Photo: It doesn't make much to attach the cell grid to a groove top bar frame. Don't try this with a wedge top bar or the cell grid will sit crooked. This is the front side of the cell grid.

Drilling a couple of holes in the top and bottom of the cell grid, I attach the cell grid using simple, ½" pan-head screws or sheet metal screws to stabilize the cell grid to the frame. Since the cell grid is not subject to excessive force (i.e., an extractor), two or three screws is sufficient.

Because the bees favor adding burr comb to open spaces, I trim a couple of pieces of plastic foundation to fill the void on both sides of cell grid. With a groove top and groove bottom board, the plastic foundation snaps right in. I measure the gap between the cell grid and the end bar on each side and cut my plastic foundation on a regular table saw.

I remove the clear panels from the front and back of the cell grid, and I insert the cell cups on the back of the unit. I think it's a good idea to go ahead and fill all 110 with the brown cell cups, even though I know I don't need that many queens.

Photo: There is no sense leaving anything to chance. Go ahead and fill up the cell grid with all 110 cell cups. The black electrical tape keeps bees in the front. This is the back side of the cell grid.

The queen is particular and will not lay eggs in every cup, for reasons no one has yet to figure out. Based on my experience, I prefer to provide the queen the opportunity to fill too many cups rather than not enough.

There is no penalty for extra eggs going unused so I fill the unit with a bounty of cell cups. The cell cups can be reused for the next batch of queens, even with old, dried up eggs.

The capacity of the cell grid provides for 110 cell cups and I extravagantly install all 110 cell cups. Go crazy! It doesn't matter if I only want to raise ten queens, I feel it is better to give my queen ample cups rather than be cheap and try to restrict her. The queen won't lay eggs in every cup, anyway, so I provide ample options for her persnickety pleasure.

Once the cell grid is attached to a frame and loaded with cell cups, I open the queen-right hive. I find the queen and hold her in a queen catcher. Because I advocate marking my queens, I seldom have trouble finding her, and by the way, darker queens are definitely more difficult to find.

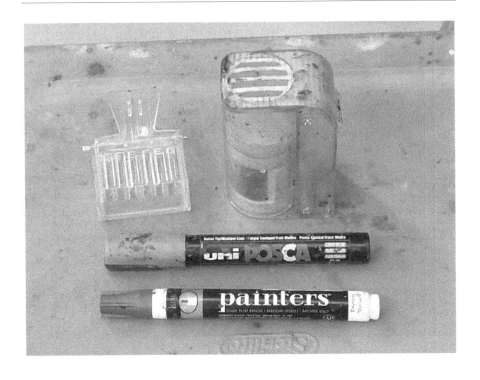

These are my essential queen marking tools.

Marking queens with the queen marking kit sold by the suppliers (sponge plunger and a clear tube) is my method, even with all my experience. There is nothing restricting experienced beekeepers from finding easier ways to keep bees, including marking queens with tools that make it easier. There are no blue ribbons for doing it the hard way.

At this point, I remove a couple of frames from the brood area, so I can insert the frame with the cell grid into the heart of the brood chamber between two frames of open brood. I prefer removing two frames from the outside of the brood nest (often ignored or filled with nectar) then spreading the center frames, creating a single vacancy in the middle of the hive body for the cell grid.

The cell grid is slightly wider than a single frame. By removing two frames, I allow myself the luxury of moving frames around to allow easier access to the cell grid without squishing or rolling bees on the combs.

But, what do we do with these two frames we removed? I bring along another brood box, put it on top of of the hive, and temporarily store these two extra frames here. I want the frames to be close at hand because we will shortly take out the cell grid after we're done transferring larvae and I want things to be simple and convenient.

It does not matter if this colony is one or two brood boxes high. I prefer to rotate or reverse the brood boxes to move the brood nest to the upper box, and make the location for the cell grid easier to access. This is not critical, just handy from my perspective.

I replace the solid, clear panel on the back of the cell grid, and leave the front side open and exposed.

At this point, there is no need for me to put the slotted, front cover on the cell grid. So I leave the front open so the nurse bees can access the cell cups.

I insert the frame with the cell grid into the heart of the brood nest and push the frames closer to it. This will create about a 1/2 frame space on the outside. Don't worry about it at this point. You'll want a little cushion of space when you take the cell grid in and out of this queen-right colony to check for newly hatched larvae.

Placing the cell grid between two brood frames gives the unit a couple of days to "warm" up and allows the workers to polish the cells cups and make it acceptable to the queen. Open brood frames are loaded with nurse bees who obsess over their housekeeping duties.

From my previous failures, I adamantly conclude this step is essential! The young nurse bees must prepare the cell cups. When other aggravated beekeepers call me, irritated at their lack of success, one of the first questions I ask is if they followed this step. Most have not and chosen to ignore it. Either they didn't know about it or they did not think it to be necessary. I preach a simple message: Do not ignore this step. The system works when you work.

I release the queen back into the hive (or in some cases, I'll leave her in the queen catcher for the next 48 hours). The egg-laying box is not yet ready for the queen. Her day comes on Day 0.

> **Side note**: Because I have to come back and recapture this queen, I've marked her to make her easier to find. To make the process of finding her even easier, I will release her into a super or a brood box that has a queen excluder on both the top and bottom, basically "sandwiching" the queen in a semi-restrictive prison. This way, I know which hive body or super contains the queen when I come back to put her in the cell grid. I've spent too many hours looking for queens, even marked queens that evaded my efforts to capture them. They run into the corners and hide out in the bottom of the hive. Sometimes, as the bees were getting aggressive from my lengthy search, I needed more smoke. This caused the bees to become "runny," that is, running all over the hive bodies. Once they get runny, it's

impossible to find the queen. Since I'm on a timetable, finding the queen on that particular, respective day is mission critical. So, to make it simple, I will begin to close up the hive by placing a queen excluder under one of the hive bodies or supers. I release the queen into this box, then top it off with another queen excluder. This way I know EXACTLY where to find my queen. Marked queens are much, much easier to find. Using a queen excluder limits the number of frames I have to remove and scan in my search for the queen. Fewer frames moved reduces the chances of rolling or damaging a queen.

I close up the hive with the cell grid in the brood nest and the queen released in a super. To avoid potential frustration on my return trip when I put the queen in the cell grid, I set the slotted front cover to the cell grid on the top of the inner cover which is under the telescoping cover. This way I know exactly where it is when I return. I need to keep it handy and setting it on top of the inner cover is ideal.

By the way, as a reminder, the back panel of the egg-laying box is solid, and the front panel is slotted. If I mess up and confuse these two covers, the NICOT method breaks down pretty quickly!

For the next two days, the worker bees clean and polish this cell grid/egg-laying box and make it more hospitable to the queen.

Giving the colony 24- to 48-hours to make the cell grid presentable to the queen is essential. Do not underestimate this step.

In the meantime, the four cell builder colonies function pretty normal. The larvae in the bottom box are maturing to the pupal stage and the queen continues to happily lay eggs in the upper box. Life is good.

Day 0:

This is the day we officially start the queen-rearing process. Everything up to this point, beginning on Day -5, was preparation. Today is the day I legitimately start raising queens.

I return to my queen-right hive and remove the frame holding the cell grid. Without worrying about the nurse bees on or in the cell grid, I place the clear, slotted panel on the front. With my hive tool, I gently remove the white, plastic plug on the dime-sized escape portal.

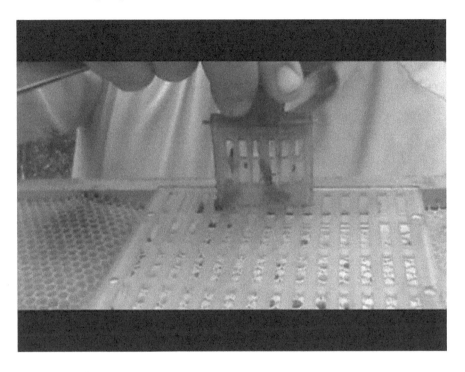

Photo: Releasing the queen into the cell grid. This is the front side, and once released, the white plastic plug seals the escape hatch. The queen catcher was spray painted with red paint, as a random color. The queen catcher kept falling out of my pocket, and in tall grass it was extremely difficult to detect. The red paint helped to locate the queen catcher and reduce a lot of profanity.

Since my queen-rearing colonies are typically gentle, I wear no veil. After removing this white plastic plug, I bite down on the plug between my teeth. I don't want any wasted time trying to find it. Yes, I'm careful I don't swallow it, and thankfully,

I'm usually by myself so I'm not answering a bunch of questions with the plug between my teeth.

I find my queen, catch her, and release her into the front section of the unit through this escape portal and close it with the plug. I cannot afford wasting time looking for the plug, allowing the queen an opportunity to bail out of the cell grid. Biting down on the plug between my teeth makes it readily available for a fast placement and the queen is secure.

Photo: The queen, as she appears under the slotted front cover, will attract more nurse bees to care for her. As she lays eggs, these bees will attend to those eggs when they hatch.

I set the cell grid back into the same place, into the heart of the brood chamber, and then I close up the queen-right hive. I now wait for the queen to lay eggs. I don't need to return until the newly-hatched larvae are found. Eggs hatch in three and a half days, which gives me an idea on when to return to transfer larvae. For this reason alone, I need to heed the schedule.

By the time the larvae hatch, it's Day 4. By Day 4, nine total days have passed since I since I set up the cell builder colony. Everything is falling into place.

Now if it just won't rain.

The queen, based on my experience, may take a couple of days before making up her mind regarding laying eggs...or not. So for one or two days, not much happens. Her majesty will fuss and stomp around the cell grid like a diva. It's like she needs to get used to her captivity before she'll cooperate with me.

Also of note: this queen may immediately start laying eggs on Day 0, but these queens are the exception. She may start laying on Day 1, or she may take two days to figure things out. As the saying goes around here, "You just can't never know, for sure."

It remains a mystery to me why the queens take a couple of days before laying, but more often than not, she will take a day or two to acclimate herself to the unit, then start laying eggs.

So I note the schedule on my calendar. I see no need to reopen and disturb the queen-right colony any earlier than four days from when I put the queen in the cell grid. Meanwhile, the four cell builders continue to happily trundle along and larvae proceeds to age as expected.

Day 4:

This day has two functions. One function brings the cell builders into the proper broodless, queenless state to receive newly hatched larvae, the process where I make the transfer from the cell grid to the cell builder colony (aka, "grafting"). The second function determines if the larvae in the cell grid are ready for transfer. It's a big day with a lot of stuff going on.

As this is Day 4, I may have larvae ready to transfer, provided my queen started laying on Day 0, maybe Day 1. But I have learned two things: first, not to count on it, and second, not to count against it. I need to keep an open mind to be flexible. But I'm getting ahead of myself.

First, before I open the queen-right colony and check on the possibility of newly-hatched larvae, I return to the four cell builder colonies. They need to be "cut down."

As this is now Day 4, I am nine days into the whole process. Remember we started on Day -5. After nine days, the bottom box in the cell builder colonies are filled with sealed brood, emerging bees, young nurse bees but no eggs or uncapped larvae. This state is what I call, "broodless."

Because I constrained the queen in the top box, I know the bottom box is "queenless." When I open each of the cell builder colonies and inspect the bottom brood box, I should have no eggs, and no open larvae; no exceptions. This way the workers will have no other option than to make queen cells out of the larvae I transfer.

If I find eggs or larvae in the bottom brood box of any of the cell builder colonies, something went wrong and I abandon all hopes of using that respective cell builder colony to produce queen cells. I pull out the queen excluder and return that colony to the stage of a normal production hive.

Despite the standard rule that claims the presence of only one queen per colony, it surprises me how many colonies have unmarked, supersedure queens running around unabated. I find some queens possess the innate ability to wriggle through the queen excluder and invade the bottom box. My first objective is to check the bottom box to insure there are no eggs and no uncapped larvae.

Ironically, back long ago in the previously disastrous seasons when I only prepared one cell builder colony, I encountered problems with second queens and other mistakes. Since preparing four cell builders anticipating and preempting such problems, I have not encountered these challenges. Maybe it's karma or Murphy's Law. Still, I prepare four cell builder colonies. They may not all be needed on every batch every time, but four colonies reduces my anxiety level going into Day 4.

The terminology of "cutting down" a colony means some of the the hive bodies are taken away, and usually only leaves one hive body. Bees on some of the removed frames are shaken back into the original, single hive body, concentrating the bees and strengthening their focus to devote their energies on whatever I desire them to do.

In this case, make queen cells. The process concentrates the worker bees into a crowded environment which improves the chances of making high quality queens. Cut-down colonies are also set up for comb honey production.

I prepare the "cut down" stage by setting up a new hive stand about ten feet away from these cell builder colonies. With four potential hives to cut down, and a new hive stand in place, the second step is to place four new bottom boards on the new hive stand. I also bring along the corresponding number of tops and inner covers. My hive stands are eight feet long and easily accommodate four hives.

The third step in the cut down process removes the upper brood box from the original hive, keeps the queen excluder intact, and retains the existing queen. I place this brood box on the vacant bottom board on the new hive stand.

By keeping the queen excluder in place on the bottom edge of this upper brood box, I insure the queen remains in the upper box, and thus, in theory, my bottom box remains queenless.

Photo: This is the same picture from before on Day -5, with the frames sorted, a queen excluder installed and the queen released into the upper brood box. It's now Day 4 and the larvae in the bottom box are now sealed and I consider it "broodless."

Returning to the bottom box on the original hive stand, I carefully inspect each frame and insure there are no "accidental" queen cells made. I assure myself there are no fresh eggs or young larvae, which is a sign of the presence of a queen.

If I find queen cells, which I do from time to time, I usually squish them. I still have an option of splitting the hive and placing each frame containing a queen cell into a new nuc box.

Photo: This is the cell builder after the cut down. In reality, I'll move the red box on the right (formerly the upper brood box) to a new hive stand about ten feet away. It sits next to the other brood box in this picture, purely for illustrative purposes. The queen and all the brood are in the red box on the right. The left box has bees, but no queen or brood so it is queenless and broodless. About half of the frames from the brood box on the right will be shaken back to the lower brood box on the left to insure lots of young nurse bees.

This is an option, actually more of a dilemma. In choosing this option to split up these frames, I limit the number of queens this cell builder raises for me. It is more advantageous if I squish the handful of accidental, emergency queen cells and allow this cell builder colony the opportunity to make ten times more queen cells by transferring newly hatched larvae.

It is, however, still my choice to squish them or to break up this bottom box into a couple of nuc boxes. After all, as I set up four cell builder colonies, I have other cell builder colonies to build queen cells for me. Free queens are free queens and the bees made me a handful of queen cells. Additionally, they are ready to go into a mating nuc right now.

Personally, I hate killing off good queen cells. When I find queen cells in the bottom brood box, I generally move on to the next potential cell builder and cut it down. If I cut down three other colonies with no accidental queen cells, I split the first one into nucs. Free queens are free queens. The bees have already done all my work for me. All I need to do is acknowledge their help and say, "Thank you!"

For the purposes of this book, I'm going to proceed as if all four bottom boxes were free of open larvae and did not contain any accidental queen cells.

The fourth step in the cut down process finds an original hive stand with four bottom brood boxes devoid of larvae and queen cells. About ten feet away, the process finds a new hive stand with four upper brood boxes which sits on new bottom boards with the queen excluder still intact. These upper brood boxes contain their respective queen.

The fourth part of the cut down process involves shaking some of the young nurse bees from the upper brood box on the new hive stand back into the lower brood box on the original hive stand. I take great care not to shake the existing queen back into the lower brood boxes or I really mess up the process.

Thus, my first objective is to find my queen in the upper brood box on the new hive stand. Remember why I wanted her marked? I remove each frame and search for the marked queen in this box, and once found, hold her in a queen catcher.

If there is no queen on the frame, presuming her to be on some other frame, I carry the frame of brood and young bees I just removed over to the bottom box on the old hive stand and shake the bees into the bottom box. This frame is returned to the upper brood box on the new hive stand.

I repeat the process and shake about half of the frames back into the lower brood box, but I don't want to deplete too many frames of young bees in the upper brood box. I need to use a little common sense and find balance between shaking frames to bolster the cell builder colony and leaving enough bees to take care of the queen.

After shaking four or five frames back into the lower brood box, I inspect the remaining frames for my queen. Once I find the queen, I remove the queen excluder from the underside of this upper brood box. If I encounter trouble finding the queen, I keep an eye on the excluder when I remove it. Often, the old queen is on the excluder trying to wiggle through and escape.

This part of the process adds additional younger nurse bees to the broodless, queenless cell builder hive, making it stronger and more efficient to raise queen cells.

I remind myself every time I cut down a potential cell builder colony to examine the frames BEFORE I SHAKE THEM to insure I do not accidentally shake an unmarked queen. Statistics vary, but the percentage of second queens in normal hives runs around 20%. The reason most of us still believe there is only one queen in a colony is because we stop looking once we find a queen. It still surprises me how few beekeepers mark their queens.

And if queens remain unmarked, how can any beekeeper know the age of the queen they find, or if the bees superseded their old queen?

It almost goes without saying that inadvertently shaking a queen back into the cell builder colony wreaks havoc and brings frustration.

Once I finish the fourth part of the cut down process, I add the inner and outer covers on this upper box. Now on the new hive stand, each upper box is ready to resume its normal functions.

However, "normal" is not really the word as this hive is weakened. It's not going to function as a "normal" hive unless I move it to my basement by the washing machine.

Nope, I'm not going to let go of that joke.

Each bottom brood box on the original hive stand is called a "cut down" hive because it has been, well, cut down in size.

Each cell builder colony is now staged to receive larvae which they welcome and feed into queens, constructing enlarged cells with great enthusiasm.

The final products are four, highly populated cell builder colonies with lots of young bees, no open brood, and no queen. The frames are filling up with incoming pollen and nectar (thanks to the field bees returning to these hives on the original hive stands).

Each cut down hive has an abundance of young nurse bees that are undistracted by the tasks of feeding larvae. There is no queen so they are looking for an opportunity to feed royal jelly and make a new queen. These young nurse bees are freed up to give their undivided attention to the handful of larvae I'm going to transfer to them. I have created the environment primed and ready to raise queen cells.

Now I also have four weakened, queen-right colonies about ten feet away on the new hive stand. Each colony has a depleted work force, an older queen, and low expectations for the rest of the year. They will act like a colony that has swarmed, except the old queen is still intact.

I generally let these weakened colonies build up for the rest of the summer as a single brood box with no supers added unless necessary, and it's seldom necessary to add supers. By the time the queen rebuilds the population, the honey flow in my area is done and these colonies are scheduled for fall management.

By fall, they have usually recovered sufficient strength for winter. Many will have superseded their queens because I've messed up their equilibrium in the cut-down process. I generously feed these colonies, especially right after the cut-down process. Since all the field bees will be returning to the original hive stand, this hive is several weeks away from being able to bring in nectar and pollen.

With four cut down, cell builder colonies in their broodless, queenless state, brimming with young nurse bees, emerging bees, incoming nectar and pollen, I move to the next part of my Day 4, the transfer of newly hatched larvae.

Chapter Eleven:

Transferring Larvae
to the Cell Builder

My next big step in the process of raising queen cells is transferring the cell cups from the cell grid in my queenright colony to the cell builder colony. I cut down my four, broodless cell builder colonies and they are ready to receive newly hatched larvae. However, I need to inspect the cell grid in my queenright colony to see if I have newly hatched larvae ready to transfer.

The ideal window to transfer newly hatched larvae is that 12- to 24-hour stage. I move the cell cups from the cell grid to the yellow cell cup holders, then fasten the yellow cell cup holders to the brown cell cup fixtures.

Photo: Brown cell cups which are placed on the back side of the cell grid. The queen lays eggs in these cell cups through the holes in the front of the cell grid.

Photo: The brown cell cups are placed on the back side of the cell grid back on Day -2. On Day 4, when the eggs hatch into larvae, I will transfer the cell cups to the yellow cell cup holder.

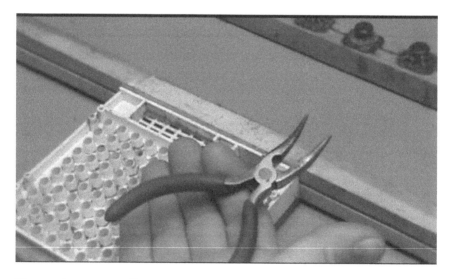

Photo: I use a small, needle-nose pliers to extract the cell cups from the cell grid when newly hatched larvae are present.

Photo: Here we are on Day 4. You can clearly see the small dot of royal jelly in the cell cup on the left, where the cell cup on the right still holds an egg. I remove the cell cups and with the needle-nose pliers and place the cell cup in the yellow cell cup holder.

Photo: The yellow cell cup holders. The brown cell cups are inserted into these cell cup holders, the cell cup holders are then pressed onto the cell cup fixtures. The cell cup fixtures are nailed to the top bar frame.

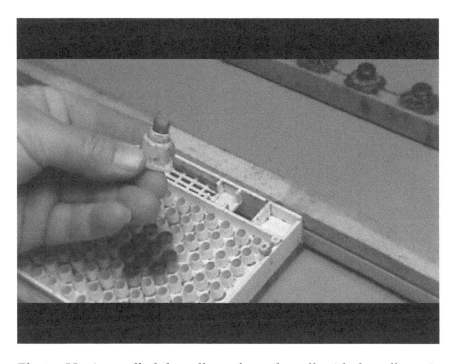

Photo: Having pulled the cell cup from the cell grid, the cell cup is inserted into the yellow cell cup holder.

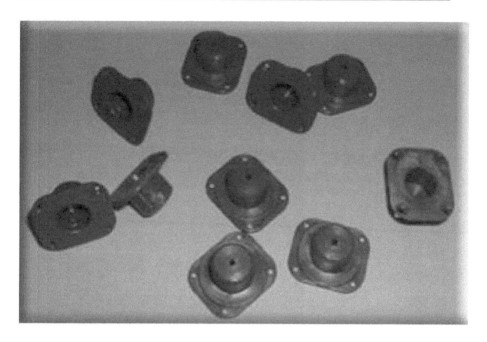

Photo: These are the cell cup fixtures which I attach to a groove top bar on a medium frame.

Photo: The yellow cell cup holder is slid, by a simple friction-fit, onto the brown cell cup fixtures. I nail ten cell cup fixtures to the groove top bar. This picture shows the top bar sitting upside-down and it will be placed in the cell builder colony with the cell cups hanging downward, ready for the young nurse bees to draw out the queen cell.

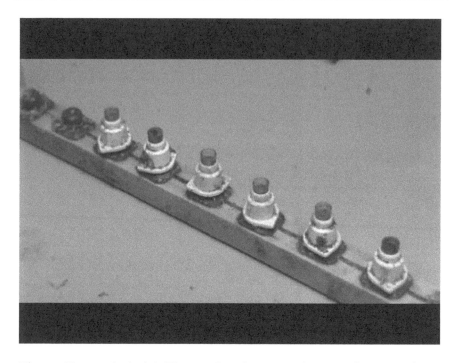

Photo: I'm optimistic! The top bar frame with everything in place, ready to be set in the cell builder colony for the purpose of making queen cells and making me a very happy beekeeper.

I transfer the cell cups from the cell grid to the yellow cell cup holders, which in turn, slide on the brown cell cup fixtures with the larva intact. This is one of the advantages of the Nicot system, namely, I transfer cell cups and not larvae. Nothing is disturbed.

Because I visibly see the little dot of royal jelly on the back side of the cell cup, I know with certainty the egg hatched and I have newly hatched larvae.

There is no guess work trying to determine the age of the larvae. It's almost like cheating.

Here is how these details work out.

Day 4, Continued

Yep, it's still Day 4, and I'm still in the detailed description of the Nicot system. I feel exhausted from explaining the cut down process, but I am only half-way toward making queens. The first part of Day 4 is to cut down the cell builder colonies and set the stage for receiving newly hatched larvae.

Once this is done, I advance to the second function of Day 4: transferring the larvae.

The schedule calls me to check the cell grid in the queen-right colony for newly-hatched larvae. If I find larvae, I proceed to transfer the larvae to the first cell builder colony.

But if I fail to find newly-hatched larvae, and if I find only eggs, it's not really Day 4. I return the cell grid to the queen-right colony and call it a day.

This is a wrinkle with the NICOT system: I have to suspend time until I find newly-hatched larvae. Day 4 is marked when the eggs hatch into larvae.

If there are no signs of larvae, it's not Day 4 but a "limbo" day in which I suspend counting the days. I revise my plans and return the next day in search of newly-hatched larvae, and if they are present, it will be Day 4, and I resume counting the days on the schedule as I transfer the larvae to the cell builder colony.

If, on this second visit, I find no larvae, it is, again, not Day 4 but another "limbo" day. I continue suspending the counting of the days on the schedule. Time stands still.

I return again on the next day after that, and in the same fashion, and I look again for larvae in the cell grid. If no larvae are present, it is yet another "limbo" day. Once again, I suspend counting any days.

This arrangement is one of the more difficult concepts to teach when using the Nicot system. I deal with the possibility of suspending the schedule for several days until I find newly-hatched larvae.

So how is this possible that I cannot find any larvae in the cell grid for several days?

Let's suppose Friday is our anticipated Day 4. Day 0 was back on Monday when I released the queen into the cell grid. If the queen laid eggs on her first day in the cell grid, Monday, I find newly-hatched larvae on Friday. Friday is Day 4 as designated by the presence of larvae.

As it is Day 4, it's time to transfer the larvae to the cell cup fixtures, and place those frames in my cell builder colony. I continue counting of days as if nothing went wrong. If the queen laid eggs on Monday, with newly-hatched larvae found on Friday, there is no interruption of the schedule Friday is Day 4. There are no "limbo" days.

But hold your horses. If the queen did not lay eggs on Monday, but waited until Tuesday, then I won't find larvae until Saturday. Eggs require three and a half days to hatch, and if the queen held back on Monday, not laying eggs until Tuesday, I won't see any signs of larvae until Saturday. Thus, Saturday becomes Day 4 because all I found on Friday was eggs. Friday is a "limbo" day. I suspend the counting of the days and pretend Friday never happened. Saturday is Day 4.

Remember, if there are no larvae, I have not yet reached Day 4. If I find only eggs, I tell myself to have patience. I put my plans on hold and return the next day, again, in search of larvae.

The unknown variable is always, "What day did the queen lay those first eggs?" Just because I released her into the cell grid is no guarantee she started laying eggs. It's something along the lines of leading a horse to water...

Or as some folks reason, "You can lead a human to knowledge but you can't make them think."

Some queens are more aggressive and some queens are just downright stubborn when it comes to laying eggs in the cell grid. I have yet to find the key to predicting which queens lay eggs right away and which ones wait. Sooner or later, the queen will acquiesce and lay eggs. I've never had a queen not lay any eggs at all

Further, the queen will not lay all the eggs in one day, normally, so I will only find a certain number of larvae on that first Day 4.

This variable is a weak-link in the NICOT system. In the back of my mind, a voice of impatience begs, "Just transfer the eggs and go do something else."

Thankfully, my wiser, inner beekeeper says, "Don't be a fool, you fool. You cannot transfer eggs. You tried it five times last year. It didn't work then, it won't work now. What's changed making you think it's going to work this time?"

I confess I tried transferring eggs on multiple occasions and it didn't work. I tried it a couple more times. It didn't work those times, either. I've had other beekeepers call me complaining how they just didn't get any queen cells built, and when I inquire if they were sure they transferred larvae and not eggs, they concede they transferred eggs.

Transferring eggs won't work. Just trust me. It may be you've waited four days according to the calendar, but if you have no larvae, you're wasting your time transferring eggs. Wait for the larvae.

So how do I know if, or when I have fresh, newly-hatched larvae? The good news is it's not hard. I open the queen-right hive and lift up the frame with the cell grid/egg laying box and lay it front-side-down across the top bars. This leaves the back side with the solid cover upward.

I gently use my hive tool and wiggle off the back cover to expose the back side of cell grid and the bottom of the cell cups. Be careful as these cell cups will fall out if you tip the cell grid back to you. Sometimes they even stick to the back cover when I pry it loose.

If I lift the frame straight up, light begins to illumine the cell cups from the front of the cell grid. Now my eyesight is declining with age.

Still, with adequate vision, I gaze upon the bottom of the cell cups. If I detect a little spot of creamy-white liquid in a cell cup, I have newly-hatched, fresh larvae. If I fail to see the spot of royal jelly, I have eggs and no larvae.

A pair of magnifying "reading" glasses really helps but I find they are not exactly necessary. If you've never seen an egg, it's about the thickness of a human hair and will be standing on end. Once it hatches, the egg falls over and the workers begin adding royal jelly.

The spot of royal jelly is unmistakable. It reveals the presence of newly hatched larvae. This is the beauty of the Nicot system. There is no guess work when the cell cup is ready to transfer.

If I am patient enough to wait as I return to the cell grid each day, I am practically guaranteed to catch the newly-hatched larvae at the ideal stage for high-quality queens.

If all I see is eggs, or if I cannot detect the little spot of white liquid, it's not Day 4. So I suspend the counting of the days. I replace the back cover, put the cell grid back in the queen-right colony, and make plans to come back the next day until I find the little spot of royal jelly. Pretty simple, right?

Suspending the counting of days is one of the disadvantages of the NICOT system. But it is also one of the most essential tricks to figuring out the system. Any method of queen-rearing works best with newly-hatched larvae, as young as the system permits.

On a side issue, I generally leave the queen in the cell grid until I'm done transferring larvae. It is not essential to leave the queen in the cell grid, but things seem to work better for me when I don't release the queen until I'm finished transferring all the larvae I want to make into queen cells.

Side Note: Now bear in mind, it's been at least four days since you placed the queen in this egg-laying box. It is possible that she laid some eggs right away on the first day. This has not been my experience, but anything is possible. You may find larvae in that 12- to 24-hour stage. They will not be large, but still easily visible and shaped like a little "comma" floating in a white dot of royal jelly. It has been my experience that my queens take a couple of days to settle down in their new confines before they lay eggs. Obviously, your results may differ. You may find nothing but eggs, in which case, you have to wait until the eggs hatch. This means you have to come back the next day, and the next day, and the next day until you find newly-hatched larvae, you now have the "real" Day 4.

At this point of finding newly-hatched larvae floating in a dot of royal jelly, the "real" Day 4 has arrived. I expect to find some cell cups with newly-hatched larvae and a majority of cell cups still loaded eggs almost ready to hatch.

Transferring larvae takes a little time and I don't necessarily want to do this work on top of the open hive. So when I see larvae, I carry this frame with the cell grid over to a shady spot, sometimes to the cab of my pickup truck, out of the direct sunlight, and begin transferring cell cups.

Photo: With my make-shift work desk (a plastic tote), I use my needle-nose pliers to remove cell cups with newly hatched larvae and set the cell cups in the awaiting top bar frames with the yellow cell cups already attached to the cell cup fixtures.

I remove the cell cups with newly-hatched larvae from the cell grid (a needle-nose pliers works best to wiggle and loosen the cell cup) and insert the cell cup into the <u>yellow, cell cup holder</u>. The yellow, cell cup holder fits into a <u>brown, cell cup fixture</u>. The brown, cell cup fixture is nailed to the top bar frame.

I previously nailed ten cell cup fixtures to the top bar of a grooved frame. This frame with ten cell cups of young larvae is where my queen cells are made. I place this frame, with the cell cups attached, in my cell builder colony.

Photo: On this first opportunity to transfer larvae, I filled four top bar frames, each with ten cell cup fixtures for a total of 40 larvae. I returned the next day to transfer the larvae which did not yet hatch on this day. Tomorrow's larvae are moved to a different cell builder.

Generally, upon finding newly-hatched larvae, I find 20 to 30, sometimes 40 cups ready to transfer, which means I need to pull out two or three, maybe four frames in the cell builder colony to make room for the corresponding frames of cell cups.

Photo: The top bar frames with newly hatched larvae, painted purple to signify their "royal" status, are placed in an alternating pattern between frames of pollen and nectar.

I space the top bar frames with the cell cups between existing frames of nectar and pollen. I do not place the top bar frames with the cell cups next to each other, rather I alternate them between frames of nectar and pollen.

I bring another brood box with me to temporarily hold the two or three or four frames I pull out. I'll set this extra brood box on top of the existing brood box until the colony caps the queen cells. It's just temporary so I don't get too excited about filling in the compliment of frames, nor do I worry about this cell builder creating wild frames of burr comb in the vacant spaces.

When I eventually pull out the top bar frames with the cell cups that have matured into capped queen cells on Day 10, I return the extra "pulled-out" frames back to the existing brood box, and that temporary brood box goes back into storage. These frames I pull out need to go somewhere handy and a temporary brood box will work for the five or six days it takes to cap the queen cells on the top bar frame.

By the way, ten brown cell cup fixtures on each frame is no magic number. When I set up the frame, ten brown cell cup fixtures fit so that's the number I nailed to the top bar frame.

There is a belief the bees in the cell builder colony will ignore the cell cups on the outer edge because the bees cannot keep these cell cups covered and warm. Sometimes true; sometimes not.

Once I transfer the cell cups with young larvae from the cell grid to the top bar frame with the brown cell cup holders, I still have more cell cups with eggs waiting to hatch.

I replace the back cover to the cell grid and place this frame back into the vacancy in my queen-right colony where it came from. I do not replace the cell cups in the vacancies on the cell grid where I pulled newly hatched larvae. Don't worry about it. It's not necessary and there is not enough time for the queen to lay more eggs.

I plan on returning the next day to repeat the process and move the next batch of newly hatched larvae to another of my cell builder colonies. The next day, the cell grid yields another set of cell cups with newly-hatched larvae ready to transfer to my second cell builder colony. I will very likely still have eggs waiting to hatch, and so I make plans to return the next day after the second day and repeat the process.

The queen should still be inside the cell grid. I leave her in the cell grid to allow the other eggs time to hatch. When I've released the queen after the first round of transferring newly hatched larvae, the workers cannibalize the remaining unhatched eggs in the cell cups. Returning the next day, I found nothing but clean cell cups and nothing left to transfer.

Yeah. It's weird. And frustrating.

So I return the next day, pull the next batch of cell cups with newly hatched larvae, transfer those cell cups to the top bar frames, and place the top bar frames in the second cell builder colony. I bring along another brood box to hold the two or three frames I remove to make room for the top bar frames.

Then I come back the next day and pull the next batch of cell cups with newly hatched larvae and transfer them to the third cell builder. I also bring a brood box to hold those frames I temporarily removed to make room for the top bar frames.

Likewise the next day I return and transfer newly hatched larvae to the fourth cell builder. I only transfer newly hatched larvae and the number of cell cups I transfer each day will vary from queen to queen, from batch to batch, which all depends on how many eggs the queen decides to lay.

As this is my last day to transfer larvae to the cell builder, I may, just for fun, fill out my top bar frames with cell cups containing eggs in the remotest of remote chances the bees find an egg hatching moments after I transfer it to the cell builder colony. It's a long shot, but I figure I have nothing to lose. Based on my experience, I gained nothing. Every single egg was cannibalized.

After the fourth round of transfers, I have four batches of queens, all one day younger than the previous batch, sitting in four respective cell builder colonies. Diligence requires a detailed schedule, which enables close tracking of the development of these queen cells in their respective cell builder colony.

If I feel I have a sufficient number of larvae going into the cell builder colony after the first or second round of transfers, I have the option to call it quits and move on. However, I remind myself not every cell is converted into a queen cell, and not all queen cells hatch. There's no penalty for making extra queen cells.

Let's look at this same process from a different angle. Suppose the queen decided to lay eggs and fill all 110 cell cups on her first day in the cell grid. On Day 4 I'll have newly hatched larvae which all hatched from eggs laid on the same day.

This is not the problem you imagine. I simply fill all my top bar frames and insert them into all four cell builder colonies on the same day, dividing the cell cups between them, evenly. Now I have four cell builder colonies making queen cells. This would be a great problem to experience!

Some of you may be thinking, *HOLY COW, MAN! THIS IS WAY TOO MANY QUEENS!*

Relax. Repeat after me: Not every cell cup becomes a capped queen cell; not every queen cell hatches; not every virgin returns from her mating flight. Queen-rearing is a game of attrition.

I do not count my queens until they hatch and return to their mating nuc from their nuptial flight. I always benefit from raising more queens than what I think I need! You'll just have to trust me until you finish raising your first batch of queens and count the number of successfully mated queens. You may be delighted; you may be discouraged. Every batch is different.

After the fourth round, I take out the frame with the cell grid and return the two frames I removed to make room for it. I release the queen and the attending workers and return the queenright hive back to its original form.

The frame with the cell grid goes back in storage or I set it up for the next round of queens from a different hive with new cell cups.

I don't worry about the empty and unsuccessful cups still in the cell grid with remaining eggs or larvae. I leave them to dry out. When I use the cell grid for the next batch, I refill the missing cell cups, set it in my queenright colony, and the workers will clean and polish those cell cups disposing of any old eggs or larvae.

Attrition Percentages

Know this for sure: it does not hurt to raise more queen cells than I <u>think</u> I really need. To think in larger quantities, to raise extra queens positions me at an advantage. More so, it's not really any more work to raise the extra queens.

Every step of the process experiences losses. It's better if I start out raising too many queens rather than wish I could magically make up the losses at the end of the process when I count how many queens actually returned from their mating flight. Then you have to evaluate which queens are best.

Ten larvae in cell cups on a frame does not necessarily mean I'll get ten capped queen cells; ten queen cells does not equate to ten mated queens returning to their respective, ten mating nucs. It's a game of attrition.

I find, on average, when I set out to raise a batch of queens in my NICOT system, the queen I place in the cell grid will lay eggs in 60 to 80 cell cups, on average, of those 110 cell cups. That's quite a large variation in that average.

Every batch varies. Weather and time of year are my biggest variables. Age of the queen laying the eggs also seems to make a difference. I can't help but say this over and over: make plans to raise more queens than you think you need!

So I transfer 60 to 80 cell cups into the cell builders and the bees convert 40 to 50 cell cups to queen cells. When I move the queen cells to a mating nuc, I end up with 30 to 35 mated queens who successfully return to the mating nuc (not all of them do!). Even then, I notice different laying patterns as some of these queens are noticeably better than others.

Raising my own queens creates the opportunity and empowers me to evaluate and dismiss the lesser quality queens. I get to choose the best and I'm not paying $25 for an inferior, mail-order queen that did not have time to develop her pheromones in the mating nuc. I don't pay $25 for an inferior queen my bees will soon supersede.

There is attrition on every level. When I inquired with a professional queen breeder about his success, he said that 80% of the grafts are made into queen cells, and 80% of those queen cells hatch, successfully mate and return to the mating nuc. That's a 64% success rate for a professional using the Doolittle method. Depending on the weather, and time of year, that percentage varies 20% either way, he said.

So, if I take his math into consideration, he might have a 44% success rate or an 84% success rate. That's a wide margin of possibilities, and he's a professional!

While your results may vary, I can't help but encourage you, again and again, to raise more queens than you think you need. When you count up the number of successful mating nucs, I will almost bet money you'll have wished you raised more queens when you started. But when you're counting up successful mating nucs at the end of the process, it's too late to conjure up more queens unless you raise another batch of queens.

The NICOT system gives me multiple opportunities every season to raise queens. So I make plans to start somewhere in May, continue through June, and maybe try one last batch in July.

A Few Summary Observations

The NICOT system is basically a "graftless" grafting procedure. Technically, I graft cell cups instead of individual larvae, which is a whole lot easier to do. The beauty of the process is the ease of detecting the illuminated larvae in the dot of royal jelly from the backside of the cell cup rather than squinting these aging eyes down into a dark cell in the honeycomb, bending my head, and twisting my arms to catch the right light.

The Nicot system gives me the opportunity to leave the larvae untouched as I transfer the whole cell cup. I don't worry about settling the larvae into new cell cups by grafting. The bees take over and do all my work for me!

While the following days are Days 5, 6, and 7 to the first cell builder, each cell builder I subsequently transfer newly hatched larvae into has a new, respective schedule, one day behind the previous cell builder. If I fill four cell builders, on four successive, subsequent days, I have four batches of developing queens all one day behind the previous batch.

This progression requires four schedules and four calendars and/or spread sheets...and it promises to monopolize a lengthy segment of my time. This segment is not a lot of hours each day, but a little bit of time each day, for about ten days. Clear you calendar before you jump into queen-rearing.

Now if I only wanted a few queens, say two or three, then I'm not going to worry about adding more larvae to each of the other cell builder colonies. However, experience has taught me to make additional cell builder colonies, and transfer more cell cups than I think I need.

One of the complaints I hear from inexperienced beekeepers who used the NICOT is this: "The bees only raised me three queens out of thirty cell cups."

Well, something obviously went wrong. Maybe you better give thanks for the three they did raise. Next time, start with sixty cell cups, and don't complain when they raise thirty-five queens. Results vary every time.

Always remember, the bees do not raise every cell cup with a larva into a queen cell. Not every queen cell hatches. Not every emerged queen finds her way back to the mating nuc following her mating flight.

Raising queens, regardless of the method, is a process of attrition. I counter the anticipated attrition by starting out with more cell cups than I need. In the worst case scenario, I put two capped queen cells in every nuc just to cover the chances that one queen may not emerge or one of the cells wasn't viable. This practice will increase your odds of your success. If both emerge, I'll trust the bees to work out their differences.

Each cell builder is queenless and broodless, but once I introduce those first frames of cell cups with fresh larvae, the colony ignores any additional larvae added to the colony in subsequent days. They don't just make more queens when I add more larvae the next day. I have yet to find an explanation why a colony does this, though I think I can find a logical explanation from a human point of view.

They put all their resources into the first batch of cell cups, set their course and ignore any subsequent batches of cell cups with larvae added in the following days. For this reason, I make up several cell builders and only add one batch of larvae.

I might also add cell builders are different as well. Some of them LOVE to make queen cells and other cell builders go about it like a lazy, old hound dog on a sweltering summer day as if he'd rather just lay on the porch than chase any rabbits out of the garden.

> **_*Side Note*_**: Conceivably, once all the queen cells are sealed, you can move them to individual mating nucs. Once they are all moved to the mating nucs, you still have a cell builder colony of young bees which is still broodless and queenless. You could, conceivably, use a different queen and place her in the cell grid with fresh cell cups and start the whole process over. With these cell builder colonies already established, you're that much further ahead in the process. You could be

raising two or even three generations of queens using the same queenless, broodless set of cell builder colonies.

A big question is how many queen cells can one cell builder handle? I don't know the answer to that question. I'm not sure it even has an answer. The quality of queen cells is a factor of good nutrition (royal jelly) for the developing larvae and adequate numbers of well fed young nurse bees to care for them (nectar and pollen). "Adequate" means having as many young nurse bees as possible, as many as that cell builder box will hold! The more, the better.

I've placed forty cell cups on four top bar frames into one cell builder colony, on several occasions. It seemed, at the time, a lot to ask of a colony but the bees built good queen cells. As expected, they did not complete all forty cell cups into forty, capped, queen cells.

With the queen held captive in the cell grid, this queenright colony may have started some supersedure cells, or they may start some in the next week. Imprisoning the queen skews her productivity, or how the workers perceive her productivity. They think she's failing.

Day 10

If everything goes well, on Day 10, I check for my first capped queen cells sealed into the pupa stage. I open the cell builder colony, pull the top bar frames, and count every capped (pupated) queen cell on the frame, even those cells still under construction and almost capped. By the time we build our mating nucs, they'll be ready.

After counting the capped queen cells, I set the top bar frames back into the cell builder and begin my plans for the mating nucs. As I may have three or four cell builders going, all one day younger than the previous cell builder, I will be making multiple trips to this yard to count each cell builder's progress on Day 10. Just warning you.

I don't expect the bees to turn every cell cup into a queen cell so I am not surprised to find empty cell cups on the top bar frame. The bees clean out some cell cups and dispose of the larvae. I'm happy with six or seven, even eight capped queen cells on every top bar frame. And then again, sometimes the bees raise all ten cell cups into queens, but sometimes just four. The number of capped queen cells I count on Day 10 tells me how many mating nucs to prepare.

Now, remember how I told you that raising queen cells is almost guaranteed to make it rain? Don't procrastinate and wait until the last minute making up your nucs. The clock is ticking. Storm clouds just over the horizon are headed your way, even if the skies are blue and clear...today.

On a couple of occasions, I found it rained so hard on the last day I had available to make up my nucs I could not get to the colonies to make up the nucs, nor could I pull the queen cells out of my cell builder colonies. The first queens emerged and killed off the other queens in their queen cells. I should've...would've...could've, but it was all too late. I had no one to blame by myself.

And no amount of profanity could appease my sense of screwing up. The whole batch of queen cells was ruined. I was back to square one.

Basically, there will always be rain delays. I raise queens in the best time of year when the nectar and pollen are abundant, and the reason the plants grow so well is due to timely and frequent rain showers. Every queen crop is at risk.

An alternative idea is to start making mating nucs as early as the bees seal first queen cells, Day 10, then gently removing the queen cells from the cell builder colony and placing them with the mating nuc. But be careful, queen cells are fragile. Conceivably, you could make the nucs on Day 9, transfer the cells on Day 10. Now we're talking about solid plans!

Procrastinator's Best Friend

The NICOT system includes another significant part, the protective "roller cages" that slide over the capped queen cell to protect it from being torn down, either from the first newly emerged queens or stupid workers who cannot read my mind and guess my intentions.

These roller cages also restrain any queens that emerge before I'm ready to put the queen cell in a mating nuc, i.e., in cases when I'm deluged with rain, followed by days of impassable mud.

I once pulled a frame of nicely capped queen cells on Day 10 and counted nine of the ten cells cups capped. Yea! I was one happy camper. I was obviously happy for nine capped cells, but I was also experimenting with some late June ideals trying to tweak my process upward to finding the elusive Holy Grail of queen-rearing. I thought I may have found it.

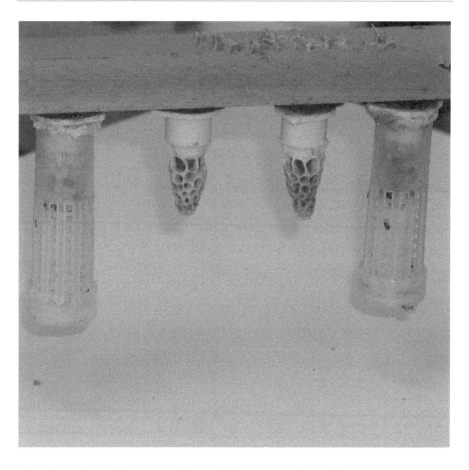

Photo: Capped queen cells and the protective roller cages to keep early emerging queens from killing other queens.

So I made plans to set up nine mating nucs. The next day I made up the nucs, Day 11, then found myself busy on Day 12 and Day 13. On Day 14, still with plenty of time to spare, I went back to the cell builder to transfer the nine capped queen cells to these awaiting nucs.

Much to my horror, I found only one queen cell remaining. The other eight cells were torn down. I responded with weeping and gnashing of teeth, plus a few choice, four letter words echoing off the tree tops. But again, no amount of profanity could rectify my frustration nor legitimately make the situation any better.

What went wrong? It was still too early for the first queen to emerge. Did I miscount the days? Was there an existing queen in the cell builder colony? I tore through each frame and found nothing. Not only did I lose eight queen cells, I lost the results from my tweaking thinking I really had found a new way to raise queen cells. Man, I was totally fuming.

Consulting David Burns from Long Lane Honey Farm on what might have happened he said, "I'm not sure. There may have been something wrong with the cells; the workers may have come to the realization that they did not need all nine cells...it could be anything."

Another lesson learned. Remember how I suggested I was not the star pupil my bees wished I was? The bees are the ultimate teacher. Never mind what I did, or failed to do, they are the final authority, judge, jury, prosecuting attorney, hangman, undertaker, and officiating preacher.

What I love about David Burns is his gentle humility when it comes to discerning seventeen possible scenarios to what I am attempting to describe to him solely from my ignorant perspective. He has no problem stating his straight-forward uncertainty given any number of variables I may have missed. And I absolutely praise his willingness to listen to me fuss and whine.

So now, on Day 10 or 11, when I open the hive to count queen cells, I slip a protective roller cage over each fully capped cell. When I give my queen rearing presentations to local associations, I call these cages, "A Procrastinator's Best Friend." These roller cages give me incredible peace of mind, not to mention a little bit of grace in a very rigid, unforgiving schedule.

If something should happen to my schedule (which is very common), if we should get thirteen inches of rain (yep, it happened once), if my kids or wife have other plans for my day, plans which "you were told a long time ago to put this on your calendar, dear," (yep, guilty as charged), or if the President of the United States offers me a night in the

Lincoln bedroom (yeah, it might happen) those protective roller cages prevent emerging queens from killing each other due to my inability to stay on schedule.

And my inability to stay on schedule has happened. And I'm still waiting for that call from our nation's capital! Whatever happens, thank you, protective roller cages!

I have noticed one other snag with the protective roller cages. When I have the top bar frame in a cell builder colony, and the queens emerge into the roller cage, I expect the bees to feed those newly emerged, virgin queens. In a normal hive, those queens emerge and start looking for something to eat. They amble over to a cell filled with nectar and take a good long drink. Six days stuffed into that queen cell can make a queen bee quite thirsty.

With the roller cages, the queens emerge and they are held captive. Sometimes the bees in the cell builder will feed these captive, newly emerged queens. Sometimes the bees ignore them.

I asked leading apiculturist from the University of Georgia, Jennifer Berry, why this was happening. She concluded, like David Burns, unsure about what was really happening and wondering if I had all my observations correct, that maybe these virgin queens did not have sufficient queen substance to attract workers to feed them. Because they smelled like ordinary worker bees, as their queen pheromones were not fully developed, these virgins were ignored and starved. Another frustration.

Roller cages cannot obliterate all my shortcomings, and while love may cover a multitude of sins, roller cages just buy me a little flexibility. The best place for that virgin is in the mating nuc, and my best success comes when the queen cell hatches in the mating nuc.

The Option of the Incubator

Last year, I began experimenting with pulling the top bar frames with capped queen cells out of the cell builder and moving them to a 93° F incubator (34° C).

This takes place on Day 10, or whenever the whole top bar gets capped. The yellow cell cup holder is easily removed and allows the transfer of completed (capped) queen cells to replace the blanks on another top bar frame so I have ten capped queen cells on every top bar frame in the incubator.

To keep these queens from running around my incubator destroying the other queen cells, I'll slip a roller cage over the capped queen cell. But I have a problem as I don't have other bees present to feed these virgin queens when they emerge.

On or about Day 15, I'll place a tiny dot or drip of honey on the tip of my finger and rub the mesh of the protective roller cage to give that emerging virgin some immediate food. I inspect my incubator three times a day to catch the virgins as soon as possible, to move them to an awaiting mating nuc as soon as possible. With every inspection, I make sure some honey is present. In the warmth of the incubator, it likes to run down to the bottom.

If I'm rolling along with overlapping crops of queen cells from a couple of hives, the incubator gives my cell builder colony a six-day head start on another batch of cell cups from another cell grid. I've only started using the incubator a couple of years ago and I think the jury is still out. Still, it provides another management option for my queen-rearing.

As I've said in my manuscript, **"Sustainable Beekeeping: Surviving in an Age of CCD,"** when we have options, we have choices. When we have choices, we are empowered to choose a path for our best possible outcome. My incubator gives me more options.

Aside from moving the schedule up six days on the cell builder, the real benefit of the incubator assures that each queen cell hatches, which guarantees me a live virgin for each mating nuc. It prevents me from inadvertently slipping a "blank," a queen cell that won't hatch, into the mating nuc.

Cory Stevens candles his queen cells and tells me sometimes those nurse bees will cap an empty queen cell as if the larva was present. He also acknowledges that sometimes things happen to that pupating queen and the larva dies in the cell between Day 10 and Day 16.

The incubator holds the queen cells until they hatch, and once I find that hungry virgin running around the roller cage, I take her out to the bee yard and slip her into an awaiting mating nuc. The key to utilizing the incubator is having the nucs ready to accept the newly hatched virgin.

Since the virgin's pheromones are not fully developed, releasing the virgin directly into the mating nuc is a perfectly acceptable option, and now my preferred method. I don't need to confine her to a queen cage until the bees eat out the candy plug, as if she was a mated queen. I also know, for sure, that the mating nuc received a live queen. There is no issue not knowing whether or not the cell hatched.

But again, the jury is still out on this practice. Using an incubator refines my management options and helps eliminate one more variable in queen rearing.

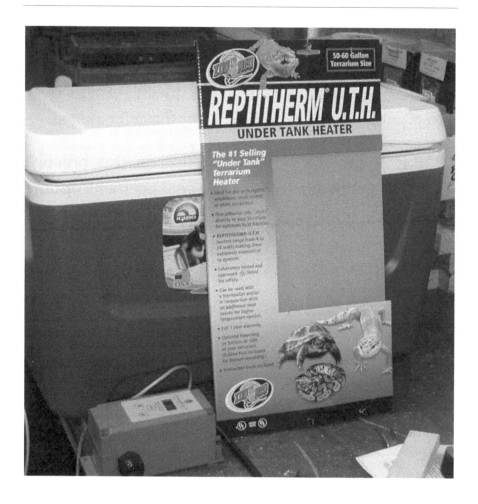

Photo: Here's the basics of my incubator. I bought a cooler (ice chest) from Wal-mart for about $18. The pet heater from Petco was about $40 and some change. The thermostat was part of my normal beekeeping junk for warming up honey.

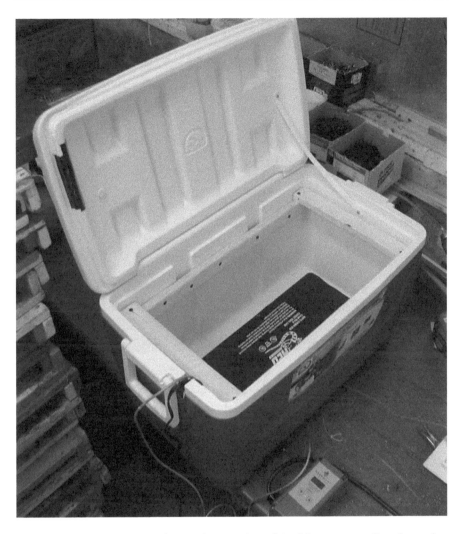

Photo: I built a simple rack, made of 1x2" scraps, fixed to the walls of the cooler with 1-5/8" sheet rock screws. This is a frame rest to hold my top bar frames of capped queen cells. I did have to cut a small notch by the handle on the left side of the picture to run my power cords and the thermo-coupler that registers the inside temp.

Photo: My top bars with capped queen cells enclosed in protective roller cages. I pull these frames, on or about Day 10 when the cells are capped, handling them very gently.

I remove any "blanks" or vacant cell cups and transfer the yellow cell cup holder with completed queen cells from other frames to finish out all ten cell cup fixtures on the frames that go into my incubator.

This cooler, with the frame rests, holds six frames or sixty queen cells.

Photo: Ten queen cells with emerging queens.

I check the incubator three times a day to insure I move those virgins out to an awaiting mating nuc as soon as possible. I am moving in the direction of "direct release" of the virgins from the roller cage to the mating nuc.

Because these virgins have not yet fully developed their pheromones, the bees don't seem to take note of their presence and I can slip them in easily without much hassle.

Direct release guarantees I have a live virgin in the mating nuc. Installing capped queen cells does not give me such assurance. Either way does not guarantee a successful return from the mating flight.

Since this practice is still very new to me, I do not know if incubator queens are any better or worse than naturally released queens in a mating nuc.

Photo: A closer photo of emerging queens. The top bar frame was painted purple, first, to make these frames easier to find in the cell builder colony (and yes, prior to painting these frames, I left one in by mistake only to have a nice bunch of queen cells ruined). Second, purple is the color of royalty! I want these larvae to know they are special and destined to be a diva! You go, girl!

Chapter Twelve

Time to Make Mating Nucs

On Day 10, I open my cell builder hives, pull the top bar frame, and count my capped queen cells. The number of capped queen cells is the number of mating nucs I need. After slipping a protective roller cage over the capped queen cell, I return the top bar frame to the cell builder colony, and close up the hive (this is my method presuming you have not built yourself an incubator). It's time to make mating nucs.

A mating nuc is just a box that allows the queen to emerge from her queen cell and be greeted by the workers who will feed her and take care of her until she makes her mating flight. The mating nuc has frames of drawn comb so the queen can begin laying eggs. A mating nuc does not have to be large, but should contain enough young nurse bees to provide the care for the eggs she lays.

Either later that day, Day 10, or the next day, Day 11, I go through a variety of other colonies in different yards and borrow two or three frames of sealed brood and young bees from each colony, then set the frames in a nuc box with the complement of additional frames of drawn comb to fill out the nuc.

Obviously, frames will have differing amounts of honey, nectar and pollen, and varying amounts of brood. I try and find frames of sealed brood, rather than open larvae. I want emerging bees to help my new queen get going. Different frames will also have different amounts of worker bees present. The section process is more art than science, quite imperfect.

If I only take two or three frames of bees/brood from a nice, strong colony, and replace the frames with new frames of either fresh foundation or drawn comb, I'm confident I will not hinder the honey production. The queen in those colonies is usually functioning in high gear this time of year.

I prefer establishing these nuc boxes in a different yard at a new location, and I don't like to set up nucs in a production yard with strong hives, or I'm asking for a robbing scenario. In most cases, robbing is not too likely if there is a nice flow on, but I've seen some crazy stuff happen to mating nucs once the flow drops off.

I also find it beneficial closing off the entrance to the mating nuc for 24 hours. I prefer a wire screen still providing good ventilation. Holding the bees captive for 24 hours, then moving them to a new bee yard the next day, does wonders for enticing them to claim the nuc box as their new home.

I find it easiest to set up the mating nucs one day, set them out in a mating yard the next day, then bring the top bar frame of queen cells to the nuc the following day. This means I need some cool or shady place or they will overheat. With two frames of bees and brood, this isn't much of a problem. Still, overheating can be an issue with any time left in direct sun.

For example, I assemble my mating nucs on Day 10 or 11 and screen off the entrance. I'll move them to a shed where they remain cool and out of the sun. Then on Day 12, I'll set them out in a new yard at dusk and remove the screens. Some bees will be making orienting flights the next morning. Day 13 or Day 14 finds me installing queen cells or releasing newly hatched virgins from my incubator on Day 16 when they hatch.

I also cut a three inch circle out in the lids of my mating nucs. I cover this circle with 8-mesh wire. The purpose is for ventilation, but this circle also allows me to invert a quart canning jar filled with 1:2 syrup (one part sugar; two parts water...very dilute). The nucs need to be fed.

Photo: My mating nucs. The frames are in the bottom (blue) box. It's hard to detect the inner cover between the brood box and the "eke" (weathered wood box under the outer cover). An "eke" is an English word meaning, "to augment." It gives me room to stack other stuff like a feeding jar on top of the inner cover, which is evident in the next picture.

Photo: I've removed the eke to expose the feeding jars on the inner cover. Two 3" holes, cut with a "hole saw" that fits any electric drill. Hole saws are readily available from any hardware store or home improvement center, i.e., Lowes or Home Depot.

A piece of 8-mesh wire, large enough to cover the 3" hole allows quart jars to be inverted, with very small holes punched in the lid for feeding. Special Note: I use normal canning lids, but I reverse the lid so the holes are closer to the 8-mesh screen.

The inner cover is simple plywood (3/8" or so) with a rim of 3/4" 1x2's around the outer edge. The sugar syrup shows the presence of my own version of "Honey-B-Healthy." The eke is cut like a brood box and it can be used as a second story to the nuc.

Photo: One of my mating yards. It receives a nice time of early morning sun and is protected with midday and afternoon shade. Of note, small hive beetles, SHBs, prefer shade. As a preemptive, proactive measure, I used some form of SHB trap in my nucs. The easiest one to use is the "Hood" trap which uses vinegar and oil. Several other options include any of the "beetle jails" or "beetle blasters" which also use oil. I'm averse to using pesticides or chemicals in my mating nucs, legally approved, or otherwise.

When I pull the capped queen cells from my cell builder colony, to safely transport the frames, I put the frames in a super containing metal, nine-frame, notched frame rests. These frame rests keep the frames secure in the super. I set the super on an upside-down lid, and enclose it with another lid on top keeping things warm and free of drafts.

Since I raise my queens in the middle of the summer, keeping them warm is hardly an issue! I've known some beekeepers who put an old fashioned, hot-water bottle in the super. May and June in Missouri are typically quite warm and humid. No additional heat is required.

When I remove the top bars from my cell builder colony, I often note several bees clinging to the queen cells or surrounding the protective roller cages. Some cells have a dozen bees clamoring about them, other cells have none.

I don't know what this means. On any given day, there are bees hanging on some of the queen cells. Then the next day, they're hanging on another queen cell. Don't read too much into this sign.

I use to be under the impression clinging bees meant better queens inside the cells. But the bees move from cell to cell so it just leaves me confused. Some days, I just have to trust the bees to what they are doing.

Transferring Queen Cells to the Mating Nuc

I remove the yellow cell cup holder with the sealed queen cell from the brown cell cup fixture and insert it into the mating nuc. With care, I gently wedge the yellow cell cup between two frames of brood. Two little tabs on the cell cup holder secure the cell cup against the drawn comb of the brood frame.

Some of these cell cup holders are reluctant to let go of the brown cell cup fixture. Removing the cell cup from the fixture without squishing the queen cell is risky. Using my needle-nose pliers again, I gently twist the yellow cell cup holder to break its obstinate hold from the cell cup fixture, then I remove it with my fingers.

Before I insert the queen cell, I remove one of the drawn frames from the mating nuc to make ample room for queen cell. I usually pull out one of the newer frames from the outside of the mating nuc as it is empty and void of nectar and brood.

As I hold the queen cell in one hand, I slide the frames closer together with my hive tool, and gently wedge the queen cell between two frames of brood. I want just enough tension and pressure to hold the queen cell. I sure don't want to accidentally squish it. I have never been able to push all the frames of brood together with the queen cell inserted, and thus I pull one frame from the mating nuc to give me a little "comfort room" until the queen emerges.

So I pull one of the empty frames and set it along side the mating nuc. Once the queen emerges, in the next couple of days, I need this frame to fill out the mating nuc, and leaning it up against the side of the mating nuc keeps it handy. Since it is empty, the only real fear I have is strong sunlight melting the comb. Robbing is not even on my radar. When I'm really organized (yeah, right) I bring an extra brood box to keep them close by and shaded.

I insert the sealed queen cells into the mating nucs and leave them undisturbed for about a week. I feed 1:2, sugar/water, so-called, "thin" syrup. I like the presence of a "feeding stimulant" often called by the brand name, "Honey-B-Healthy®." There are three commercial formulations of this lemongrass and spearmint oil mixture on the market, available from any of the major suppliers.

If you do not move your nucs to a remote yard apart from a production yard, any feeding stimulant attracts robbers. Not so much of a concern in May or

June, but anything later in the season in my former corner of southeast Missouri was tempting disaster of a monumental scale. Our natural nectar flow normally shuts down right after the 4th of July in a normal year...but trying to define, "normal," has no basis in reality.

If I insert the cells on Day 13, I'm in good shape, but as we all know, "stuff happens." Queens emerge on Day 16 and I do not want them emerging in my cell builder colony because, "something came up," with my schedule.

Inserting cells on Day 13 is ideal. Just the intention of getting this accomplished on Day 13 gives me a nice leeway of a couple of days, but there is no room for procrastination. If I catch a 36-hour larvae, which sometimes happens on the first batch of larvae I transfer on Day 4, they will actually be a day ahead of my schedule and will emerge on Day 15. Do not leave important details to the last possible moment.

I am also a man not unacquainted with the difficulties of controlling unforeseen emergencies and interruptions. That's another HUGE reason why I insert protective roller cages on Day 10. I cover my contingencies. I buy a little flexibility and it's cheap insurance.

Obviously, when the ripe (unhatched) queen cells go into my mating nuc, the protective roller cage is removed. When I'm releasing virgins, I take the roller cages with me, remove the inner cover, and allow the virgins to walk out of the roller cage and down into a couple of frames of bees and brood. The direct release of virgins doesn't require the removal of that extra frame to allow her room to walk in.

A week after setting up the nucs, it's Day 20. I quietly open the mating nuc, pull apart the frames, and gently slide out out the cell cup holder with (hopefully) the empty queen cell. Then I move the frames together, and replace the extra frame I previously removed. The hive is put back together and I continue feeding the nuc. This move allows me a moment to inspect the queen cell to insure it hatched. If not, I mark this nuc for another queen cell.

Queen cells have a "trap door" on the bottom of the queen cell that slides shut, sometimes, after the queen emerges from her cell. It may look like the cell didn't hatch, but by Day 20, if the cell didn't hatch, it's not going to hatch. Something went wrong. So on Day 20, when I pull the yellow cell cup holder out of the mating nuc, I give the trap door a little flick of my finger nail or hive tool.

Sometimes I find a dead queen pupa inside, yet a couple of times I released a pent-up virgin who said, "About time! Who makes these things so tight you can't get out?" How she lasted so long is beyond me.

Not every queen cell hatches, which is something I've mentioned from time to time. Again, asking my resources of expert queen producers and teachers why this happened only begs more questions as to many various variables and possibilities.

Sometimes, when I've got more queen cells than mating nucs, or I'm running out of time, I'll put two queen cells in a mating nuc just to cover my bases. Should two queens emerge, I let them work it out.

Photo on the left page: Holding the queen cell by the yellow cell cup holder, I flicked open the trap door with my finger nail. Success!

Was the Mating Flight Successful?

After emerging on Day 16, a queen takes roughly 5 to 7 days to mature. They go on their mating flight and it's another 3 to 5 days before they lay eggs. I usually figure by Day 28 (five weeks into the whole process when you begin on Day -5) I can inspect my mating nucs and look for larvae and fresh eggs.

Just to keep my schedule simple, I inserted the queen cell on Day 13. One week later, on Day 20, I pull the yellow cell cup holder with the (hopefully) hatched queen cell and reassemble the nuc. One week later, on Day 27, I check the nuc for eggs. If the queen emerged and successfully mated, this day is the earliest time to inspect my colonies.

If I see eggs, I find the queen, and mark her. If there are no eggs but I see the queen, I give her one more week to settle down and finish her business. I return and inspect the nuc on Day 34.

These days in the process, Day 13, Day 20, Day 27 and, if necessary, Day 34, will fall on the same day of the week, and will make my personal schedule easy and theoretically uncomplicated. I still have to deal with weather issues interrupting my schedule.

If I fail to find fresh eggs, my queen may not have mated and returned to the mating nuc. Things happen under a large umbrella of "attrition," and sometimes the nuc begins to make their own emergency queen cell, usually a dead giveaway my queen failed.

One of the reasons I like making up my mating nucs with sealed brood is to avoid the construction of these accidental emergency queen cells, but frames often have small patches of new eggs which are not easily noticeable when I make up my mating nucs.

General consensus deems these nuc-raised, emergency queens inferior because the nucs lack large populations of young nurse bees to adequately feed and nourish quality queen cells.

Generally, I mark any suspect or failed nucs for a new queen cell, but until I have a new queen cell ready, I may allow these accidental emergency queens to emerge. Sometimes the bees know how to do things better than the "experts" give them credit for, and sometimes the season is getting late and I may not have another round of queen-rearing planned. My other option is to get on the phone and purchase a mail-order queen. I prefer to leave well enough alone and let this inferior queen emerge.

Locating Mating Yards

A big question is where to place my mating nucs, hopefully in a different or remote yard other than my yards with production hives, as I've already mentioned.

I've used different locations just for the sole purpose of setting up mating nucs. As these nucs need to be fed, holding them in one location is just plain convenient. Sometimes I leave them in this yard to overwinter, and then move them to more permanent locations for the honey flow the following year.

There are a series of studies on Drone Mating Zones (DMZ's for all of us not involved in the Korean War) or Drone Congregating Areas (DCA's). There are several reasons why drones choose certain areas, landmarks, and topography. Dave Tarpy from the University of North Carolina has excellent resources on drone behavior.

One thing to remember, that many queen producers forget, is that a virgin queen will fly two miles to separate herself from her brothers from her original hive. Drones only fly a mile or so. And with my generous populations of feral colonies in our area, almost anywhere works for me. I have a network of bee yards within reach for mating.

Photo: I think we forget that 50% of the future of our hives and their honey gathering productivity or defensive behavior against the mites comes from the genetic contribution of the drones.

Drones, my "studs," in plentiful numbers from a diversity of hives, is the key to my mating success. Since queens are open-mated, there is no way to insure which drones or what race/strain inseminates the queen. Still, I try and insure my hives have lots of drone comb in an attempt to raise my odds for a good mating.

The irony becomes when I take this mating nuc and move it to a new yard. The virgin emerges, presupposing the drones in that yard are the sons of her mother, so she'll fly away to a different area, which may just be back in the flight range of the original queen-right colony from which the larvae was transferred back on Day 4.

I don't try and over think the relationship of the location of my mating yard to other apiaries in the area. But I do want a lot of available boyfriends in the area. I will add drone comb to the colonies in the area, but I also trust in our large populations of feral bees.

I favor using one bee yard for my mating nucs, a yard that sits in the middle of four other bee yards which surround this location, all two to five miles away from this mating yard.

I believe this gives me the best option for my queens finding drones, wherever the drone mating zone materializes. Centralizing this mating yard also concentrates my nuc inspections and saves me time and energy.

Drones

Just a quick note on drones. The queen will mate with 18 to 20 drones on her mating flight. With a diversity of colonies and lots of feral colonies, I lose a great deal of genetic control with the open-mated process. But since I'm producing locally-adapted queens, I'm hoping I'm mating to locally-adapted drones from surviving colonies, whether managed by me or feral colonies in the woods in my area.

I receive a great deal of questions from new beekeepers hoping to minimize the feral component of the available drones. They come at queen-rearing as if they were raising purebred dogs or crossing two breeds of cattle for a desired hybrid mix. But the reality is the queen mates with whatever drones are out there, from whatever colonies are in the area, from whatever drones find her and catch her.

I've heard from some beekeepers who raise queens to give to their neighbors down the road so the neighbor won't be flooding the drone areas with chemically-addicted, medication-dependent, mite-susceptible, inferior genes. Now that's smart! It also makes you a great neighbor.

If you raise queens in an area with Africanized Honey Bees (AHBs), I suppose you could flood the area with your own drones from various colonies in a mix of apiaries by placing special frames of drone foundation into hives surrounding your mating yard.

But it's still a game of Russian roulette, or in this case, African roulette, and there is no accounting for feral colonies or where the queen flies away to mate.

If there is any good news, healthy colonies produce drones. Once again, I find myself at the mercy of nature and the natural selection around me to give me some good drones.

One other word or warning, it is the drone's genetic contribution that determines the temperament of the hive. If you have a colony of hostile, hot, aggressive, and defensive bees, do not hesitate to raise queens from this colony just because they are not gentle. Do not get upset when you raise queens from a gentle hive and those queens turn out to be as mean as a snake with a belly-ache. It's the drones. Their genetic contribution is the wildcard in queen-rearing and responsible for a colony's disposition.

If you have a hot hive, requeening with a mated queen is highly recommended. Or you can move those colonies out of your back yard. I have remote production yards where I will relocate nasty hives as I don't mind aggressive bees. They are great honey producers. I just don't want them creating problems with my neighbors.

It's still debatable why hostile hives seem to be more productive, but one researcher suspects beekeepers do not routinely inspect hot hives, and when beekeepers leave hives alone, they are more productive than hives which are frequently opened (and disrupted).

Mating Nuc Success

I temper my expectations so I'm not surprised with anything less than 100% success in my mating nucs. Sometimes queens get lost on their mating flights. Sometimes they are eaten by birds or hit by windshields on passing cars. Sometimes they return to the wrong mating nuc. Sometimes the cell never hatches.

I continue to raise more queens than I need or want. Queen quality after the mating flight varies.

Conceivably, I could devise some way to gauge their productivity and cull out the inferior queens. But with my extra bee yards and desire to produce more honey, I'm not limited by the number of hives so any live queen is hired. Sometimes I am pleasantly surprised how they climb that ladder to success after an initially slow start to their careers.

Splits and Nucs

When I raise queens around the first of June, I'll have a nice batch of queens ready for my post-harvest splits in mid-July. I split my production hives and combine additional frames of bees with my nuc and the newly mated queen. Laying queens are almost always accepted. The easiest way to join a nuc to a split hive is the newspaper method.

The split portion of the production hive is queenless and topped with a single sheet of newspaper. I set another brood box on top of the newspaper and add my frames from the nuc box into this brood box, I then add additional frames filling out the box. The theory suggests by the time the bees chew through the newspaper, they have become acquainted.

Other nuc producers will tell you no newspaper is necessary. They suggest a slight misting of the split hive with sugar syrup prior to combining the nuc.

I think I prefer the newspaper method.

With the queens I produce in July and August, I usually build up these mating nucs into singles for the rest of the summer into fall. I add frames of drawn comb to round out the necessary extra frames as I expand the nuc into a ten/nine-frame single brood box. I strengthen weak nucs with frames of brood from other hives.

As we usually have a nectar dearth in the late summer, I have no problem feeding theses late nucs syrup and pollen substitute patties for the simple reason there are no other resources available. I encounter many beekeepers who will vociferously argue against the practice and wisdom of feeding these artificial diets.

I overwinter these colonies as singles, mostly (maybe a "story and a half", which is usually a brood/med super) and this entails some extra management issues.

One thing I learned is to close off screen bottom boards on singles as winter approaches. Larger hives have no problem surviving with open screen bottoms, but nucs and singles need a solid bottom to survive in southeast Missouri.

Additionally, I can go back to any of my existing colonies failing to live up to my expectations, kill off the old, lackluster queen, and add a queen cell straight from the cell builder colony and skip the mating nuc.   Or I can split this colony into two mating nucs for two queen cells.

If I'm done raising queens and have no further use of my cell builder colonies (which happen to be queenless and broodless), I can use those frames for mating nucs or simply insert a queen cell into them and convert them to a large mating nuc.

Chapter Thirteen

Key Points of the NICOT System

I speak at conferences and teach queen-rearing using the NICOT system. It works for me, doesn't require grafting, and has become my bread and butter despite the NICOT method languishing in relative obscurity.

For many years I offered my notes in a PDF file, which was the initial motivation for this book, thanks again to Bob Graham, as I shared in the beginning.

Over the course of several years, my advice offered on some of the beekeeping forums on the Internet brought several inquires and questions, mostly via e-mail. I am more than happy to answer questions and you can contact me at grantfcgillard@gmail.com

Hopefully, this material answers many of those questions and puts them in the proper context. Still, I always feel like I may miss something, so if an issue arises, do not hesitate to send me an e-mail (which is the best way to reach me). In this chapter, I bring the most commonly asked issues which frustrate NICOT users.

Your success with the NICOT system hinges on a couple of key points one must observe. Ignoring these points brings frustration, mild profanity, and the erroneous conclusion that these plastic contraptions don't work. They work if you follow these essential points. The system works when you work.

First, you must place the cell grid into the queen-right colony to "warm up." The warm up period allows the workers to inspect the box, polish the cell cups, and what one queen producer suggested, "to allow the cell grid to absorb the smell of the colony."

I'm not sure of the last idea regarding any "smell," but the cell grid has to be introduced for a minimum of 24 hours, though 48 hours is better. The warm up period allowing the worker bees to polish up the cell cups is like putting on some romantic music, chilling a bottle of an exotic wine, dimming the lights, and lighting a few candles setting the mood for the queen to eagerly agree to lay eggs in the cell grid. Make her feel special like she's being courted.

Second, when you introduce the queen to the cell grid on Day 0, she might lay some eggs the first day, she might not. If I was a gambling man, I'd bet she won't lay her first day. She might balk and wait two days before laying any eggs. You can neither predict nor guarantee when she will start. You can only pull the cell grid from the queen-right colony, gently pull off the back cover and inspect it on Day 4.

If all you have is eggs, come back the next day. The absence of newly hatched larvae suspends the days. Day 4 marks the presence of newly hatched larvae and the count resumes, but ONLY when newly-hatched larvae are present.

Before transferring any cell cups, you will have to inspect the cell cups to determine if the egg has hatched. With the Nicot system, this is very easy to do. The cell cups are almost clear and determining if you have an egg or a larva is so easy, any visually-challenged person can raise queens.

Third, do not transfer eggs to the cell builder colony. I have had no luck at all, not even when I transfer the last batch of larvae to the cell builder and

I need to fill out the remaining yellow cell cup holders with cell cups. Since this is the last batch, I'll pull some cell cups with eggs "just in case" the workers in the cell builder might possibly want to make them into queens. They never do. The cell cups are dry and clean when I come back on Day 4. Do not bother transferring eggs.

Fourth, as I've mentioned before, go ahead and raise more queens than you want by adding more cell cups than you think you need. The queen will not lay eggs in every cell cup in the cell grid, anyway. If you only put in ten cups, she may only lay in two. Prior planning prevents poor performance and avoids problems down the line.

As I like to leave my queen in the egg-laying box for the duration of my larvae selection process, she may lay an extra egg or two in some of the cups. Don't worry about this as the cell builder will sort it out.

I asked David Burns about the idea of taking a toothpick and squishing the extra eggs in the cell cups. He suggested I refrain from this practice as the bees in the cell builder colony will, "smell death and destruction and they'll totally avoid that cell cup."

When David Burns uses the word, "totally," I give him my full attention. David Burns is the new "E. F. Hutton" for our generation. When David Burns speaks, people listen (if you're old enough to remember those commercials).

There have been some cases where I removed the queen from the cell grid when I first saw eggs (on or about her second day in the cell grid) and as I waited for those existing eggs to hatch, the workers entered the box, and in the absence of the queen, cleaned out the eggs.

Yeah, that was a bummer. You'd think they'd get with the program. Maybe they were hoping I'd get with the program. Confining the queen to the cell grid makes for an artificial wrinkle in the balance of the colony.

Fifth, my calendar is based on how many days it takes to get things ready, including the set-up for the cell builder colony. For this reason, I start with "negative" days of preparation. My "positive" days directly correspond to the days of the egg/larvae/queen cell development.

I figure about five weeks covers the whole process from start to successful finish, from preparing the cell builder colony to finding a successfully mated queen in the mating nuc.

If I start around the first of May and raise a couple of crops by the middle of June, by the early part of July I know which queens are successfully mated so I can begin making splits.

Chapter Fourteen

Some Last Notes

I have fallen in love with some of my queens and I wanted to raise several batches of daughters just like her.

After raising one batch of queen cells from this favorite queen, I refilled the cell grid with new cell cups and put the cell grid back in the queenright colony to "warm up," this, after releasing the queen for a little respite, giving the queen-right colony a 48-hour period to polish up the new cell cups. The second time around, however, the dynamics of this hive changed with that queen confined to the cell grid for the first batch.

Invariably, the second batch never got off the ground. I continued to find empty cell cups, whether the queen simply would not lay or the workers cleaned the eggs out. I'm not sure why, but it's one of those things about the NICOT system that just doesn't work.

So after running a queen through the cell grid and transferring cell cups with young larvae, I simply turn her loose into the queen-right colony and allow her to resume her duties.

I also find, either during her confinement or right after I release the queen, some (but not all) colonies build a few supersedure cells. Apparently, the queen's confinement, not surprisingly, upsets the balance of the hive and the bees know it. Sometimes I ponder if the hive may have had plans to supersede the queen anyway, even if I had not confined her to the cell grid.

I have consigned myself to finding a good queen, using her to raise some larvae for me to transfer, then turning her back to the hive to let the bees figure things out. In most cases, she'll be replaced. Maybe it was her time anyway. I raise most of my larvae from queens that have proven themselves in the previous season and survived the winter.

Raising that second batch of queen cells from that same queen is really not in my best interests, anyway. I continue to try and diversify my queen genetics to cover all my bases. If I have a good queen, I'm tossing her into the cell grid and produce some daughter queens. Then I look for a different queen and raise another batch of queen cells for more diversity.

If I'm ready for a new round of queen-rearing, I refill the cell grid with new cell cups, ignore all the old cups (some with eggs, some with aging larvae, some empty), and start the process over in another queen-right colony and a different queen. With the 24- to 48-hours of "warm up" period, the workers clean and polish the cell cups. In this case, the bees reuse the old cell cups and clean out the dead larvae and dried up eggs.

Once the cell builder colony converts the larvae into capped queen cells, there's just too much wax and propolis to reuse them. They're cheap enough when you buy them in bulk, anyway. Any empty, rejected, or vacant cell cups removed from the top bar frame are usually sufficiently waxed that they will not work in the cell grid.

Believe it or not, I once tried to use hot water to clean out the wax and reuse the cell cups. My water was too hot. The plastic cell cups warped in the hot water. I now buy my cell cups in bulk and toss away the rejected cups from my yellow cell cup holders.

I can't help but reinforce this idea: Do not underestimate your need for queens. It is better to have too many. You can then judge the queens, kill off the lesser quality queens, and combine that colony with another one before the end of summer. This allows you to retain only the best queens. Or you can sell those extra queens or give them away to your buddies. You can even sell off your extra queen cells if you can catch them before they hatch.

And from my experience, you can never tell when an old queen is going to give up the ghost, die or go downhill just far enough to compromise the colony, but not far enough where the colony will supersede her. There's no penalty for having extra queens on hand ready to rescue a failing colony.

This short book is a description is how I do it. Glean the good stuff and make your own adjustments. I hope this little chat we've had has been helpful. I have no pretentions that this is the only way to raise queens. It's what works for me. If you have any questions, my contact information is at the end of this manuscript.

The early pages of this book list other publications I have for sale that might be of interest to you. Thank you for your considerations. I hope they bring you added success.

Feel free to contact me, either by snail or by the preferred e-mail. The NICOT system is not the easiest, nor necessarily the best, and it's very possible I've left something out as I've tried to describe the process in sufficient detail so you can follow it.

I hope to hear about your successes!

All the best,

Grant F. C. Gillard
1259 SW 600th Rd
Holden, MO 64040-9103
grantfcgillard@gmail.com

###

About the Author:

Grant F. C. Gillard began keeping bees on the family farm in Glenville, Minnesota, after graduating from Iowa State University in Ames, Iowa, with a degree in Agriculture in 1981.

While in his sophomore year, seeking the easiest class possible to raise his battered grade-point average, Grant ignored his advisor's derision, and enrolled in a seemingly innocuous class entitled, "Entomology 222: Beekeeping," taught by a retired high school biology teacher and adjunct professor, Richard Trump.

Without realizing this potentially providential twist in his academic life, Grant was hopelessly inoculated with the desire to keep honey bees including visions of commercial aspirations.

Grant was active during his high school years at the First Presbyterian Church in Albert Lea, Minnesota, ordained as an elder. Returning to his home church after his college graduation, Grant's church members, along with the Rev. Elmer Bates, convinced him he'd make a better pastor than a farmer. Their encouragement spun his life in yet another direction, but the bees were not merely a passing fancy.

In 1987, Grant graduated from Fuller Theological Seminary in Pasadena, California, with a Master's of Divinity degree. It was there he met another Presbyterian student, Kansas City native, Nancy Farris. They married in 1986 during their last year at Fuller.

He later obtained a Doctor of Ministry degree from Aquinas Institute of Theology in St. Louis, Missouri, in 2000.

Grant combined his passion for beekeeping with his pastoral duties at the First Presbyterian Church of Jackson, Missouri. At one time, Grant operated around 200 hives and produced honey for local retail sales and farmer's markets in southeast Missouri. He also produced nucs, raised queens and removed swarms. Grant is the founder of the Jackson Area Beekeeper's Association.

Grant has also published several articles in the American Bee Journal regarding colony management techniques. "A Ton of Honey: Managing Your Hives for Maximum Production" is one of his most noted books. A complete list of his books can be found by running a simple search for his name on amazon.com.

Grant is past-president of the Missouri State Beekeepers Association, serving as president during the years of 2010 and 2011. He is a frequent regional and national conference speaker. He received the Missouri State Beekeeper of the Year Award in 2012.

Grant is married with three grown children living in the greater metro area of Kansas City, Missouri. His wife of 33 years, Nancy, has taken an increasing role in selling honey at the farmer's markets.

In 2018, after twenty-five years of pastoring the First Presbyterian Church, Grant and Nancy relocated to Holden, Missouri, to be closer to their family. They also moved the bees and went to work rebuilding, rebranding and re-establishing their deep commitment to apiculture. Grant still does a little preaching at the New Horizon Presbyterian Church in Odessa, Missouri.

You may contact Grant for your next conference at: grantfcgillard@gmail.com or try and text him at 573-587-1623.

While he has been known to hang out on Facebook, he feels he squanders entirely too much time arguing with the trolls and keyboard beekeepers (the one who are all veil and no smoke).

Special thanks go to my late father, Jack F. C. Gillard, (1928 - 2012), whose inspirations always gave us children permission to be anything we wanted to be, to do anything we wanted to do, that with the right amount of hard work, with a good education and God's help, anything was possible.

I hope to pass along that same inspiration to my children.

.